THE CHURCH IN THE MARKET PLACE

The Church in the Market Place

GEORGE CAREY

MOREHOUSE PUBLISHING
Harrisburg, PA

Library of Congress Cataloging-in-Publication Data

Carey, George.
    The church in the market place/George Carey.
        p. cm.
    Reprint, with new introd. Originally published: Eastbourne:
Kingsway, 1984.
    ISBN 0-8192-1562-7
    1. St. Nicholas (Church: Durham, England) 2. Church renewal
—Church of England. 3. Church renewal—England—Durham.
4. Durham (England)—Church history. 5. Carey, George. 6. Church
of England—Membership. 7. Anglican Communion—Membership.
I. Title. BX5195.D88S265   1991
283'.42865—dc20   90-25405

Fifth Printing, 1994
Printed in the United States of America

Contents

Foreword

We have embarked on a new decade – a decade all the churches are calling a 'Decade of Evangelism'. Let us make no mistake about it, this decade could conceivably be one of the most critical of decades in the history of Christianity. Why is this so? Well, we look around and see the advances of secularism, the invasions of new forms of paganism and the insurgence of Islam and other faiths. Christianity no longer has a monopoly in our land; we are in the market place of religions and no faiths and in a real way our back is up against the wall.

So: despair? No, never! Rather a wonderful opportunity for the church of Jesus Christ really to be his church; open, alive, radiant with faith and hope. I know that churches can grow and my expectation is that we shall.

I am so glad that my little book is being reprinted yet again. It is the story of one church and our discovery that our God may be trusted. It shows the pain we went through, the changes we had to adjust to. It was not easy—but it was so worthwhile. May your experience be similar.

GEORGE CAREY
1990

Preface to the Second Edition

I am delighted that because of public demand this book is being reprinted again as there is considerable evidence that it has been of help to congregations contemplating change and renewal.

The re-issue of the *The Church in the Market Place,* however, gives me an opportunity to offer some suggestions as to how it might be used by a congregation or Church Council.

First, please note that the central emphasis falls on spiritual renewal. Don't attempt any change in church life—buildings or otherwise—without looking at the prayer life, the worship, and other elements that make up the spiritual temperature of your church. It is also important to have a large view of Renewal. This book represents some of the ingredients I regard as crucial and they still continue to guide and influence me—but I am not arguing that my style, or the particular direction that St Nic's took at that time, is necessarily going to be right for you. The only guideline I would offer is this—let your controlling principle be Christ and his will your delight.

Second, if change in any form is planned, set mission and outreach before you as your primary goals. We are not here to play ecclesiastical games, or to have warm, comfortable buildings for our sake, but to extend the kingdom of God. Therefore it is important to clarify the purpose behind the proposed changes and you will want to ask:

What should be our priorities where we are?

How essential is it for us to have modern facilities?

Does our present church building—pews, heating, lighting, etc—hinder or help our mission to those outside?

Third, try to be proactive rather than reactive. What I mean is this: so often the church reacts to problems instead of taking the initiative. We need a new roof or a new heating system and cry, 'Help! What are we going to do?'

Remember this: to God there are no such things as problems: each is an opportunity. Our problem creates an opportunity for him to break in with his power and his grace. If it is not too irreverent to say, sometimes God must sigh with relief and say to the assembled archangels: 'At last St Michael's in Much-Binding-in-the-Marsh is waking up! They are actually talking about spiritual renewal and even contemplating forming prayer groups.'

You may have been driven to this book because your church has a problem. It might be for major repairs or some pressing need. Well, now is the time to be proactive and to think about the opportunities before you. So you will want to ask questions like these:

Is God calling us to die? Perhaps our mission is at an end and it is time to recognize it. Remember that we have no divine right to exist. The church of God can never die, but the local church may if Christians are disobedient and so apathetic that they are actually dead already but don't have the sense to lie down! So, is there any evidence that God is closing down your 'shop'? No?

Good, then let us go on to consider, 'All right, we have to raise that £50,000 or so for the organ but let us now be imaginative and see what else we can do. Is it not possible, for example, to double the sum and give the rest away for missionary work,' or, 'Perhaps we should add to the scheme a centre for young people or a lounge for meetings.'

And, remember: people will give more to imaginative schemes than to tired old pleas like: 'Help us!' We need your money otherwise our church will fall down!'

Fourthly, the story of *The Church in the Market Place* is the story of ordinary people finding that God's power is available and his grace is all-sufficient. It has been amazing to meet up with others who have passed through similar situations and to hear them say, 'We met opposition like that also!' Or, 'I was so glad you wrote that book because it almost exactly mirrored our experience.' But not only will you find an overlap between the experience of St Nic's and your own, but I can promise you that you will find the ever-sufficient resources of God available. 'Jesus *is* the same yesterday, today and for ever', and, as our American friends say, 'You'd better believe it', because if you don't you will never encounter the God of the New Testament who still blesses believing and reckless faith.

Since leaving St Nic's I spent five very happy years as Principal of Trinity College Bristol and helped to raise £420,000 towards the renewal of College buildings. Many of the lessons learned at St Nic's came into play again. Now that I am Diocesan Bishop of Bath and Wells my task is still the same: to lead the people of God forward in service and action in the power of the Holy Spirit and in obedience to Christ. I do so hope that this book will be of help to you as you seek to do that too.

GEORGE CAREY
1988

Preface

This book is the testimony of a church. It was my privilege from 1975 to 1982 to serve the people of St Nicholas's, Durham, as Vicar. During that time we experienced the greatness and goodness of God as we launched out on a remarkable act of faith. It dawned on me gradually that this is a story to be shared—to encourage other Christians to enlarge their vision of what God can do. I hope it will, therefore, help churches who are grappling with issues of renewal in theology, worship, ministry and mission.

It is also an honest book. It is the true story of a church's doubts as well as its faith, its weakness as well as its strength. Because it is written from my own perspective at the centre of the church's leadership, it inevitably conveys my own reactions, fears and feelings as well. It is my humble hope that this will not detract from it, but contribute to the powerful story of a fellowship which found itself caught up in a painful period of change.

My only regret is that there are many fine Christians whom I would like to have mentioned, but space does not permit this. To all the congregation, named and unnamed, this small book is dedicated.

Finally, how can I express adequately my appreciation

of Eileen for her support and encouragement? The book will make clear her important role alongside me in the story which follows. And both of us want to thank our children, Rachel, Mark, Andrew and Elizabeth, who went 'through the fire' with us. That they did not get 'burnt' is testimony to God's gentle care.

GEORGE CAREY

St Andrew's Day 1983

1

Renewal

In 1972 my spiritual life was in a mess, to put it mildly. I was at that time teaching Christian theology at St John's College, Nottingham, a leading evangelical college which trains men and women for ministry in the Church of England. Perhaps I had spent too long in theological education, I don't know, but whatever the reason I knew that my spiritual life was at a crisis point. My heart hadn't kept pace with my head. Sometimes when I was teaching New Testament theology, I found myself thinking: 'You hypocrite. You don't really believe this, do you?' But I was trapped. I had to go along with the show. I couldn't let the side down, I had to pretend all was well.

The feeling of spiritual emptiness, or disenchantment, was especially acute when I gave a series of lectures on the Holy Spirit. I recall vividly the time I lectured on Paul's doctrine of the Spirit. The words in Ephesians 1:13 challenged me especially: 'You have been sealed with the Holy Spirit who is the guarantee of our inheritance.' I was uncomfortably aware of the gulf between Paul's triumphant assurance and my spiritual poverty. I found myself asking: 'Paul speaks of the Spirit as a guarantee, something of which he was sure, but that is just not true of my life.' All I was sure of was my spiritual void or 'ennui'.

7

In myself I was fairly normal. I wasn't a psychiatric mess, a quivering bundle of nerves or anything like that. I was thirty-seven at the time, a normal balanced, healthy person with no personal experience of clinical or patho-logical depression. I was happily married to Eileen, a marvellous person, and we were blessed with four delight-ful children. But the experience of Christianity had somehow disappeared from my life. The great truths of evangelicalism had lost their fire and their power to convince. To all intents and purposes I was all right, but I knew that if God did not intervene soon my whole Christian existence was finished. It was that desperate.

To make matters worse I was faced with a growing number of young charismatics at college whose assurance, ebullience and Christ-filled lives mocked my impoverished spirit. Three chaps stood out in particular, Brian, John and Pat. When I contemptuously dismissed their theo-logical basis for their doctrine of the Spirit they would meet my arguments with love and smiles, as if to say 'you'll learn!'

I did learn in a most unexpected way. That year we went as a family to visit relatives in Ontario. While I was out in Canada I did a spot of preaching and teaching, all the while haunted by the same spiritual emptiness. One Sunday, I was invited to preach at Little Trinity Church, Toronto, and I was kindly given accommodation in a house nearby that was shared by a number of Christians. I noticed a book on the bookshelf by an American writer, Robert Frost, entitled *Aglow with the Spirit*. 'The same kind of charismatic rubbish,' I thought as I skimmed through a few chapters—"two-stage" nonsense about receiving Jesus in conversion and then receiving the baptism of the Spirit later, ugh!' I tossed the book away in disgust, but as I did so I found myself asking, 'Hold on, it's easy to toss a book away, but what you can't dismiss is that man's joy and faith. Why are you so sure that you have nothing to learn? Perhaps God wants to meet me and fill me with his Spirit!'

It was a point I hadn't raised before but the sheer poverty of my life contrasted with what I had just read about the quality of New Testament Christianity forced me to face up at long last to my crisis. I found myself on my knees saying: 'Lord, you know the mess I am in right now. And yet I owe you so much. I thank you that you met me years ago when I was a lad of seventeen. And I thank you that you called me into Christian ministry and empowered me for your service. But Lord, I have become so busy in your service that I have lost you somehow. I have been so self-centred and interested in doing what I want that I have forced you out of my life. I cannot live a hypocritical life any more. Unless you fill me again with your Spirit, I cannot go on!' Such was my prayer, and nothing dramatic happened—no thunderclaps, no wind, no fire; but it was 'Elijah-like' because God spoke to me in a still small voice. In the calmness of that Sunday evening there was an amazing quality of peace about the room. It may sound trite, but it was so true that in that peaceful atmosphere Christ came again into my longing life and claimed me as his own.

There was only one unusual thing: a distinct word came echoing into my mind over and over again: *Shamayim*, *Shamayim*! What did it mean? Later it was to dawn on me—of course! *Shamayim* is the Hebrew word for heaven. And that evening was a foretaste of heaven, a lovely knowledge that in a simple way I had encountered the Spirit in a real way and I was home again.

What difference did it make? A great deal. It restored me to a great love of Christ, a deep desire to read the Scriptures, a longing to share the Christian faith with others and a desire to praise God. I was later to learn that these are characteristics of the work of the Holy Spirit in the charismatic movement, but I wasn't conscious then that I was caught up in a contemporary movement of the Spirit. All I was thankful for was that at last my theology had a living soul. The dying embers had been fanned by the Spirit into a fire and I was on the move again!

And the difference showed. On my return to college the first student I met was Pat whose first words were: 'Eh, George, what's happened, there's something different about you!'

The sequel to this is one of God's lovely jokes. A few months later, I attended a Theological Staffs Conference at Queen's College, Birmingham. I had to chair a discussion group and in my group was John Gunstone, a well-known charismatic Anglo-Catholic. I felt a strong urge to share my experience with John. He was delighted with the way God had dealt with me. He said in characteristic fashion: 'Look, let's pray about this. If I think it is right, may I lay my hands on you?' And so John prayed and spoke in tongues as he laid his hands on me. To be truthful while that was happening my sense of humour was uppermost, because I thought it was incredibly funny that an Anglo-Catholic theologian was laying hands on an evangelical theologian and speaking in strange tongues! And yet it was a wonderful confirmation of the transaction that took place a few months earlier. I thought, 'How like God to bring someone from outside my tradition to minister to me!' That time with John was to be a very important step in my growth because it made me take seriously the ecumenical movement; that God is working through his Spirit in all the traditions. The Spirit had started his deepening and broadening work within my life.

This personal incident (which up to now only a few friends have known) is of the greatest significance to the story that follows. Without that experience of the Spirit I am sure that the story of St Nic's would not have happened in the way it did, not because I am significant, but simply because I would never have had the spiritual resources to lead the congregation, neither would I have had insight and vision to see God at work in the fellowship. God had to make me usable.

It was two years later that Eileen and I made the decision to go to the historic church of St Nicholas's, Durham — a decision that turned out to have consequences far beyond the expectations of anyone involved.

2

Your Church Is On Fire!

'Would you like to consider going to St Nicholas's, Durham?' asked the voice at the end of the telephone. We knew next to nothing about Durham, except that it was a remote spot in the North East of England. We knew even less about St Nicholas's, although we were aware that the Rev. George Marchant had had a wonderful ministry of twenty-two years there; but the rumour was that it was rather run down now. 'Yes,' I replied, 'we'd like to see it. We feel our time is over at St John's and we are ready for a parish.'

As we approached Durham city on that glorious Wednesday in November 1974, we fell in love with the place immediately. It wasn't how we had imagined it to be—dull, grimy, and grim. We found an attractive place bustling with life. The grey towers of the cathedral towered over the town. The slender spire of St Nic's in the town square seemed fragile and helpless alongside the might and majesty of that splendid cathedral. The two church wardens gave us lunch and shared the needs of the church. As we talked with them about the parish of St Nicholas we got more and more excited about the possibility of working there. Gerald and Dick, the two wardens, were very frank about the problems of the church. 'We have a very happy fellowship,' they said, 'but we have lost some of our families to a neighbouring charismatic church. We definitely don't want an intense charismatic, or a deadly dull evangelical, but we do need a new leader. Many of our younger families and our students are anxious to see change, but we don't want a divided church. What is your vision for us if you were to come here?'

'Well,' we said, 'we would want to build on what God has been doing here. The church is obviously situated in the best position in the town. But nothing will really change unless the church family is renewed. I would want to start with house groups and gradually build up the life of the fellowship.' And then we received a reply which went to the very heart of St Nic's problem: 'We have tried house groups without any great success. We are the kind of congregation which comes together on the Sunday for teaching so that we might be topped up for our work during the week.' Our reply was definite: 'There is no future in petrol station Christianity—using Sunday to fill the spiritual tank for the week is not New Testament Christianity. Unless the church is prepared to meet regularly in fellowship and to grow closer together, it will not fulfil its mission as a church.'

We accepted their invitation to join them, and on July 17th 1975, I became the Vicar. The formidable nature of our task became clear on the evening of my institution. There must have been only about one hundred and twenty local people there. At institutions normally people turn up in their droves—if only out of curiosity to see the new Vicar! Where were the people? Was this all the congregation? Many of the congregation were embarrassed about the low attendance. 'The problem is,' they said, 'we are really a student church. Once term is over, our numbers are quite small.'

The Bishop of Durham preached the sermon at the institution and, unbeknown to himself, proclaimed a prophetic message which was to linger in many minds for the years that followed. His sermon was about 'the church in the market place'. He called for the church to be available to people, to stand for the message and ministry of Jesus, to be a holy and welcoming people of God, to be open to all that God wanted to give us. If we knew then how that inspiring vision was going to be so wonderfully fulfilled, we would have leapt for joy and gladly would have accepted all the sacrifices that were to come. But as in so many aspects of Christian work, God never allows us to peep behind the curtain of the future. We had to go through the pain and toil of faithful witness until the church was truly a church for the market place.

Another, mildly prophetic, word was to be uttered by Michael Baughen, then Rector of All Soul's Church, Langham Place, who was later to become Bishop of Chester. He and Myrtle and their family were travelling north on holiday and had coffee with us shortly after the institution. Michael shared with us their experience at Holy Trinity Platt, when the church there went through a period of growth. 'I'll tell you this,' he remarked with a broad smile, 'during your first year you can do nothing wrong. In your second year you can do nothing right. And in your third year it will all work out all right!' Broadly speaking he was right. But if we had known how bad and how long that second phase was to be, perhaps we would have gone back to the security of the theological college!

The problem was knowing where to begin. There was so much to attend to. The church building needed urgent repair and there was need for a new boiler; many were clamouring for changes to the worship; there were no fellowship groups. Where do we start? What was clear was that there were folk in the congregation praying for renewal. For them at that time it was not charismatic renewal—it was a deep hunger for God's Spirit to work among us and to bring about a change in the congregation that would lead to the whole body rediscovering its mission to the world around. And yet, as a number of us were to preach later, this is indeed charismatic, because if the gifts and graces of the Holy Spirit do not end in a growing witnessing church which makes an impact on the world around, then that church does not deserve to be called charismatic.

Renewal begins with prayer. And that is where we started. At our first Sunday services, we announced weekly prayer evenings at the vicarage every Friday evening. Those evenings were to become very precious times for us all because we learned to wait upon God in intercession and we discovered the importance of praise. The numbers were from many points of view disappointingly low—rarely more than twelve—and I must say there were times when I felt very disgusted with a congregation which had such little appetite for God's work. A verse often flashed through my mind from Revelation 3, the risen Christ's condemnation of the Church of Sardis, 'You have the name of being alive—but you are dead.' But those who came regularly shared with us the longing to see St Nic's fulfil its enormous potential—whatever that might be. What *was* God going to make of us? The ministry of prayer was a seeking and, in a way, a finding too.

Looking back on those important times in the 'parish room' of the vicarage we can see now God's faithfulness in surrounding us with men and women who were longing for a new work of God's Spirit. There was, of course, the shadow of St Margaret's Church looming over St Nic's. A few years before, this church, which was more Catholic in tradition than St Nic's, had 'gone charismatic'. The Rector, Stephen Davis, had experienced an amazing 'baptism' in the Holy Spirit and in his usual enthusiastic style had quickly introduced his congregation to this new phenomenon. It quickly caught on and many came from other churches to join that fellowship which manifested so many gifts recalling the New Testament era. Some left St Nic's prior to our arrival, including the lay chairman of the Church Council, so a history of suspicion, even a slight hostility, blocked the way to discussing what we might learn from this new movement in the church. The congregation of St Nic's clearly needed to be more open even to the possibility that the renewal movement had something to give to us in our situation.

Another great concern was worship. After our first Sunday when I had led the services in accordance with the usual practice of St Nic's, Eileen fumed and exploded. 'I'm not sure I can put up with this diet,' she exclaimed, 'it is so boring. How can we expect God to bless us when there is no joy and no life! I might have to go to St Margaret's occasionally!' And she was right. The services were largely Prayer Book services—greatly loved by the older members of the congregation particularly. But they were so very, very dull, and I realized with a heavy heart that something had to be done here also. This concern was shared by many in the congregation. Before we arrived, there had been a Day Conference at which it was resolved that modern songs and new services would enhance our worship, but nothing had happened. I quickly got a hymn book supplement going and typed myself about a hundred modern songs and gradually introduced them into the services. Didn't Michael say that for the first year you can do nothing wrong?

There was a tremendous groundswell of appreciation and love that made these changes acceptable. Again, if we knew that this was but the lull before the storm we might have been a little more circumspect in trying new things! But a number of us in the church knew that the issue was more than a mere question of jazzing up the worship—the problem was one of mission. There we were in the heart of Durham with a style of worship that was lifeless and unattractive.

The choir was an example. There were six members when I arrived; faithful people who loved music and wanted to serve God in this way. It consisted of three ladies and three teenage girls. It wasn't their fault the choir was so small. No one wanted to join them and they became a valiant, but discouraged group. I did not exactly endear myself to the choir when I changed the time of the Pathfinder group from the afternoon to the morning, which meant that the three girls went to that instead—leaving just the three ladies! Two of them were an encouraging and spiritual force in the church. The other lady in time was to leave—unwilling to accept the changes that had to come.

With the encouragement of many of the folk in the congregation I began to introduce modern songs into our services. Tom, our organist, was most agreeable and willing to try anything out. He had lovingly caressed the beautiful three-manual organ which he himself had installed twenty years before. But Tom, in spite of his enormous generosity of spirit, was not greatly enamoured with the style of music I was introducing. What I began to experience is the age-old problem of delicate relationships between incumbents and musicians. I believe I was right then to establish what I think is the correct policy for church growth and renewal. The minister must control the worship. Once others have responsibility for choosing or selecting hymn tunes and other parts of the service, the control of worship passes from the hands of the minister into that of the choirmaster or organist. The minister would indeed be foolish to ignore the help of his organist, especially that of someone who was as caring and loving as Tom. But it is still a fact of spiritual leadership that music is an element within worship and it needs to be under the guidance of the spiritual leader or leaders. Thankfully Tom and I had a marvellous working relationship in which he was able to accept new directions, if not always happily, at least supportively.

And then Veronica popped up in the congregation. Veronica was a newcomer to Durham and had just settled down at St Nic's. She was a lovely bubbly Christian. 'We must really do something about the singing,' she exclaimed. 'Look, my instrument is the flute and I am an indifferent guitarist, but I am willing to have a go.' And so our music group was born. Ken, her husband, joined in valiantly, but as he couldn't sing, his value was limited to being an encouraging presence alongside Veronica. A few other singers were in time to join, including Chris and Sally who were eventually to lead the music group on into a fine ministry. But the beginnings were small and the discouragements were great. We persevered because we were convinced that change was essential.

And then I met Wilf. He helped me to make an important decision concerning the church. St Nic's was right in the centre of the town, with literally thousands passing its door each day. It distressed me greatly that the church was only open on Sundays when the town was virtually dead, and shut when the city centre was bustling with people. I was assured that it was necessary to close it because of the problem of vandalism. Horrifying stories were produced as reasons for keeping the church closed. My instinct for an opening welcoming church clashed with my responsibility to protect a vulnerable building.

Ten days after taking up my post, I had to take a funeral service in church. After the service I went, as is the custom, with the hearse to the local crematorium and after the cremation returned to the church. In the meantime the church had been open. When I went in I found an elderly, unshaven gentleman standing before a picture of Christ at what we used to call the 'Children's Corner'. 'I am Wilf,' he announced. 'You are the new guvnor here, aren't you? I'm glad you've opened the church. This picture of Jesus means a lot to me. When the church used to be open I often came in here, just to talk to him.' On the spur of the moment I arrived at my decision. 'Wilf,' I said, 'I can promise you that as long as I am here this church will be always open. I'll do all I can to make this church available for all who want to find Jesus. Will you join me in praying about this?' Solemnly Wilf and I knelt for prayer and prayed for the ministry of St Nic's as a place where people might pop in and find an oasis for prayer.

Wilf was an ordinary Geordie working man, but on that occasion he helped me clarify my policy about the church. It was a risk, of course. Some of the older folk were unhappy about leaving it unmanned because of the danger of damage. There were times when I went down to lock up at the end of the day only to find that something was broken, or someone had tried to break open the offertory box, but those times were rare. What was more distressing to me and to Mrs Simpson, our cleaner, was when people abused the church in more distasteful ways. There were times when I had to remove human excrement from the church as well as cigarette ash and rubbish. My anger at this desecration had to be brought into line with an acceptance that service entails risk. I gradually learned that cleaning up such foul abuse of a place I loved could be a lowly symbol of my relationship to Christ. If he was willing to subject himself to human conditions for thirty-three years, this distasteful chore was something I could accept as a small gesture of love to him. Indeed, at times like that I often reflected on the example of Francis of Assisi who was told by the Lord to 'build his church'. Francis took this literally at first and virtually restored an old ruined chapel to become a glorious place of worship. To identify in a small way with Francis and more particularly with the Lord, was for me an inspiring way of coming to terms with the invasion of sin into this building.

But what was most thrilling was the way that the church

was beginning to be used in spite of its coldness and dampness. There were times when I popped in to find people in prayer or people in distress needing help. I longed for the day when the congregation would be committed enough to man the building regularly.

One day I found this note on the Holy Table: 'Dear Father, I have sinned against God. I have done the most terrible things. Please help me, pray for me.' This cry coming from the depths of someone in acute need, moved me with considerable force. How could I help this person in some tangible way? I hit upon the idea of writing a note to him, leaving it in the same place. In my letter I gave some words of advice enclosing a simple booklet. Over a period of a few weeks our notes passed from one to the other, until one day he never wrote again. I don't know what became of him, but I hope I helped him while I could.

But I do know what became of Harry! Harry was one of our tramps who hung around outside the church. I got to know him quite well when later I became Chairman of Durham Cyrenians—an organization that cares for tramps and homeless people. Harry was a tall, cadaverous figure, who shambled around the town smelling evilly. But he spoke in a most cultured way, intimating a good background at one time. He claimed to have a faith in Jesus and a love for the church, but it did not stop him trying one on if he could get away with it. One day I had just finished a Holy Communion service for the Mothers Union when one of the ladies ran into my vestry exclaiming, 'A tramp has just run off with the offering!' I rushed out and, sure enough, Harry was just leaving the church with the collection. I chased him with great determination, but old Harry showed me a clean pair of heels. I never saw Harry or the collection again. But poor Harry passed away in a most spectacular fashion. Jim, one of Durham's mayors, told me that one evening Harry went into the Town Hall for a cup of tea and he dropped dead at the Mayor's feet. Harry obviously enjoyed making a dramatic exit, no matter what he was doing!

But opening the church in that way revealed the deficiencies of St Nic's as a place of fellowship. The roof was in urgent need of attention. Mrs Simpson had six buckets handy and when it rained she placed them in the appropriate places in a brave though vain attempt to control the flood. Sometimes in the services we could hear 'plop! plop! plop!' as a rhythmic beat to accompany our singing. This combined with the bitter cold of St Nic's meant that you either had to be singularly committed to the church to come regularly for worship or singularly hot-blooded! We seemed in those early days to be constantly fighting against the elements. We faced the problem of either the leaky roof or the wind whistling across the square, driving such warmth as there was through the gaps around the windows and through the roof.

Then there was the boiler. St Nic's must have been the last church in the whole of the diocese still to have a solid fuel boiler. Every Friday evening or Saturday morning, Jim, Mrs Simpson's son-in-law, would light the boiler and over the weekend make frequent trips to keep it going. This meant that smoke and fumes very often filled the church. It was sometimes so bad when I went down early on a Sunday morning to take the eight o'clock service that I had to leave the doors open to clear the air. The result, of course, was that the cold air replaced what little heat there was before! On two occasions the policeman on duty in the Market Square phoned me to say: 'Sir, smoke is coming from your church roof—we think that your church may be on fire!' On the second occasion with great longing I replied, 'No, Officer, it's not, but I certainly wish it were!'

One Saturday, the boiler just would not light. Jim called me in great panic: 'I can't get it to start! It has always lit before. I can't understand it!' We quickly got other experts in and we coaxed it with a wide range of fuel and tried every trick in the book—but it refused to oblige. To this day we do not know why this happened. I wondered at the time if it had anything to do with the new pathway that the civic authorities had placed alongside the church, but that did not really explain why the boiler should suddenly decide to call it a day.

The upshot of this was initially very grievous, and in the long run very thrilling. It meant that for much of our first winter in Durham the church had no heating at all. We did the best we could with six calor gas heaters which the cathedral kindly lent us. My part-time colleague Graeme Rutherford and I collected these heaters every Saturday night from the cathedral and returned them the following evening after our last service. That period stands out in my mind with all the force of a nightmare. Never have I lived through such a black period of discouragement. The sheer physical labour of those frequent trips lugging heavy heaters into my tiny car one by one, together with the worry of having such a cold uninviting church, was an emotional drain which threatened to overcome our usual high spirits and optimistic outlook.

But God is able to redeem the blackest situation. We clearly had to do something about replacing the boiler and we found that the best model would cost £2,000 at least. For many churches this would not have seemed a very big sum, but for St Nic's then it seemed beyond the resources of the congregation; it had never raised anything like such a large amount before. In 1975, the congregation almost trebled its gift day figure by giving £500 for the vicarage kitchen! So we had to turn the problem into prayer, and it was wonderful to see people viewing the matter as a spiritual challenge which had to be faced. And to everyone's great surprise—and my relief—over £2,000 was given and the boiler was put in, to the great benefit of all. Mind you, there was not a great improvement in heat because the problems of the building were too enormous for a boiler to be the answer. But it was at least an improvement on what we had. The real significance, however, lay in the fact that we had begun to give *sacrificially*. Admittedly we had a long way to go, but we had passed our first real test.

I saw this incident as a little parable of renewal. St Nic's was a place of good faithful Christian men and women who loved their Lord and their church. Some of the younger folk longed for change, but it was becoming more and more clear that, until the fire of the Holy Spirit was at the centre of our church life, very little could be done. His warmth had to be generated by a fellowship fired by him, and until we allowed him full possession we would remain cold and useless. We needed to replace the old boiler of relying upon our own resources with a new one—the power of the Holy Spirit.

So after nine months we were in a position to look more objectively at our situation. One thing was clear: the church was visibly growing in number, our services were more joyful, and people were learning to give generously. But with that happy assessment there was also a sombre realization—the storm clouds were gathering and we were about to enter our second year. Michael's second phase was about to be astonishingly fulfilled.

3

You Have Destroyed My Church

She stood in front of me, thin lipped and quivering with suppressed anger. 'I have never experienced such a hullabaloo in all my life. I have worshipped in this church all my life and I hope this morning's scenes will not be repeated!'

It's not every Sunday that a Vicar gets comments like that after a morning service. Mrs Lee was referring to our monthly Family Service which we had just enjoyed. And enjoyed was the word. Why should worship be dull and boring? If it is as important as we believe it is, should not Christians attempt to make it as pleasurable as possible? This was our philosophy behind the Family Service. We had introduced a very simple liturgy which with modern choruses, lively singing and an illustrated talk we hoped would meet a real need in the congregation. As a result the monthly Family Service had begun to grow. But it clearly did not please Mrs Lee. 'If this continues, you will not have my support any longer.' One of the church wardens overhearing this outburst was very worried. 'I'm afraid, George,' he said, 'that that complaint is not isolated. A number of people are very unhappy by the changes in worship, but they are afraid to approach you directly.'

What we half expected was now a reality. Opposition! At no point had we introduced anything against the wishes of the Church Council. Indeed the partnership between myself and the lay leadership of the church was excellent. We were agreed that changes in worship were essential. They were very supportive and encouraging, even though it was my responsibility to take direct action. We had tried to make the changes as gently as possible, but it was clear that we had arrived at a crucial point in the church's progress. Either we stopped and possibly even returned to the familiar securities of traditional worship, or we pressed on with our programme of renewal.

Over the previous few months, a number of us had tried to show that in no way were we trying to destroy or remove the Prayer Book. But, I argued, beautiful as it is, it is no vehicle for reaching the outsider or for touching young people. 'I like it too,' I said to many, 'but it is not a question of what I or you like, but whether the language of the Prayer Book can reach our contemporaries or even express the spiritual devotion of modern Christians. The church is not a religious club whose only responsibility is to its own members. Our worship is a shop window to the world. If our worship is attractive as well as reverent, joyful as well as devotional, relevant as well as anchored in Scripture, then God will use it to draw many to him.'

So with this philosophy before us we fashioned our services to express our love and worship of God. Our Friday evening praise and prayer meetings began to focus on worship, praying that it would be beautiful for God and would draw many to him. As with so many other areas in the Christian life, the irony was that just at this point when some were complaining about the introduction of new elements, others were expressing their pleasure about a new sense of God consciousness there was in our services. 'I didn't think you could ever enjoy worship!' exclaimed one younger lady. 'That song we sang this morning really spoke to me,' said another. 'I really look forward to worship now,' was yet another comment. The consensus of the church family was that the changes were greatly appreciated.

And then the letters started to arrive. Letters of complaint, letters of distress, angry letters and sad ones too. And Eileen and I began to feel the waves of panic as we read sentences like, 'I am sorry that I no longer feel that I belong at St Nicholas's Church.' 'Dear Vicar, there used to be such peace at our church, but now it all seems so noisy.' Of particular sadness was one written by the wife of one of our senior lay folk which said: 'Dear George, I know that you have acted from the highest of motives in initiating change and we all appreciate the love and care that Eileen and you give. But you have destroyed my church and I can never forgive you for that. I find it impossible to worship there any longer.'

Eileen and I had great affection for that lady and her family. Long before we arrived in Durham their children had drifted away from the church, and now it seemed as if we were driving her away. Again, if we knew that she would eventually come back into fellowship and that two of her children were to find a living faith through the renewed church, we could have found comfort and encouragement in that. But all we could see at the time was that our plans for improving worship were dividing the congregation.

Over the summer of 1976 we received more than thirty such letters and experienced the pain that all in Christian ministry know—the pain of having to do things which distress others. And it is a pain that one cannot share with others, however supportive they are, because they are not associated with the changes in the way that the actual leader is. At least Eileen and I could share the pain together, and this taught us a lot about the importance of a shared ministry. The sadness came, of course, from the fact that we cared very much for these dear people. It was their church before we arrived, and now, as it must have seemed to them, through the whims of a new vicar their faith was being shaken to its very foundation. One lady described it in a not too pleasing way: 'It's like someone coming into my favourite room and turning it into a saloon bar!' Not the best of analogies perhaps, but the statement denotes the kind of turmoil that people were feeling.

Over that summer, Eileen and I were kept very busy simply trying to explain what we were trying to do and why the changes were necessary. We felt at times as if we were holding onto a disappearing congregation! Yet through it all we knew we had the support of the majority of the Church Council. All except four or five knew that such progress had to happen.

Then came that fateful evening in July. I had just returned from a meeting in London and was really looking forward to an evening at home. Eileen greeted me with the news; 'Jean would like you to pop around to her house this evening for a short while. I think you have trouble. She has invited a handful of people, all of whom are concerned about the changes in worship.' I groaned inwardly because this really did spell trouble. Jean was one of the minority on the Council who did not approve of what was going on. I wondered what was in store.

When I walked into Jean's lounge, I was taken aback by the number of folk packed into the small room. Over twenty, mainly elderly people were there sitting in a tense, embarrassed silence. I tried to make conversation, but it was hard going. My attempt to engage a few with a smile met with averted looks.

Stephen, another Council member and a well loved and greatly respected member of the congregation, began by saying: 'George, I have been asked to chair this hastily convened meeting. A number of the congregation think that you are making so many changes that they feel excluded from their own church and no longer belong to it. No one denies that you have done a great deal of good, but some are alarmed by certain aspects. We want you to listen to us and our concerns. After we have finished there will be a chance for you to speak.'

As I sat there I was aware of a rapid succession of emotions. The first was a feeling of detachment from it all, as if it was happening to someone else. This may have simply been the natural reaction when one's ministry and leadership is under attack. This feeling was replaced by a momentary feeling of despair. Is renewal of the church possible, I thought, when one has the opposition of such defensive people? Jostling with that went an initial reaction of anger that some Christians could be so wilfully opposed to what was so obvious to most of us.

Yet I think God gave me a more enduring feeling of compassion for those stalwart people who were so fearful of what God was doing and who now clung to the past with the tenacity of a drowning man clutching at anything that offered hope. Silently I prayed that God would enable me to listen keenly to what was said, and that he would make me a real pastor to each one of them.

And for over an hour the list of complaints, worries and objections were aired and shared. Some were said in the heat and fury of the moment—voices raised in anger, citing instances of bad worship experiences. Some complaints were said hesitantly by people trapped between what they wanted and what they felt younger people wanted. At last my ordeal was over. 'Well, George, thank you for listening,' said Stephen sympathetically. 'We have about ten minutes before we must stop. Do you want to respond?'

But what could be said after these outpourings of such fears and anxieties? It would have been only too easy to meet argument with argument, but that would not have helped. Our differences did not lie in worship, love of God or anything like that—the difference between us was one of vision. They saw no reason to change—I saw every reason to change. But what could I say that might bring us closer together?

It says in Scripture that Christians faced by difficulties will find that the Holy Spirit will answer for them. So it was that I found a real freedom in the Spirit to share very simply my vision for a renewed St Nic's serving Christ and a needy world. 'It is not my intention to destroy our church,' I said. 'I know you are concerned and I appreciate the frankness of tonight's meeting. It must be difficult for many of you to come to terms with new services, strange new songs, guitars and so on. But what I want you to observe is that the church family is growing, isn't it? Isn't that what it is all about? Can we really be happy with a church that is indifferent to the thousands who pass our church doors each day? I think we all realize that when the Holy Spirit starts to work in a congregation there is always change and pain and ragged edges. I really do believe that the Holy Spirit is going to do a mighty work among us. Be patient and let us work together for the glory of Christ.'

I led them in prayer and left, feeling sad, empty and discouraged. I was glad I had a supportive wife to share this with. We were depressed together; anger, sadness, hopelessness and love mingled together as emotions which we offered to God to purify. 'How can they be so blind!' stormed Eileen, angry at the incident.

But both of us knew that it is only too easy for Christians—all of us—to shut our eyes or close our ears to new truths and fresh opportunities. Those dear folk at St Nicholas's were not alone in the land in refusing to allow God to address them in new ways. It is a recurring problem. One thing we were sure of: we couldn't go back. The Spirit of God was beckoning us forward, and we had to obey.

But the bad times were not over. Far from it. Over that summer, meetings were called after services and ding-dong arguments ensued. Eileen often found herself in the firing line because she ran the Mothers Union branch, and some of the most hostile objectors were members. It is difficult when one is going through such a black period to believe that any good will come out of it. There were times when the easiest solution would have been to toss in the towel, return to the monochrome worship of the past—and to an easier life!

But thank God there was always the support of others which made the bad times sweet. There was, for example, Jenny. Jenny is a lovely Christian lady now in her seventies who makes exquisite marmalade and strong ginger wine. Our joke about Jenny's ginger wine was that it was the most effective paint stripper on the market, but we always came back for more! Jenny was and still is regarded as a dear and kind Christian lady whose whole life is a witness for Christ. Jenny was a tremendous support. 'Don't worry, Vicar,' she would say. 'They'll learn. Just carry on preaching Jesus.' How we all need Jennies in our ministries— real saints of God with the Barnabas gift of 'perking' people up.

There was also Miss Bulman who was ninety-one at the time. A frail lady, her memories of the church went back to the 1890s. But she did not dwell in the past. She was delighted to see the congregation growing and only too pleased to see the church trying new things.

Evelyn, one of our two choir members, was another quite fantastic person. She was also getting on in years, but she didn't show it. She had had a remarkable career as a local business woman, but had also experienced more suffering than most people. She had lost her only son in a swimming accident, lost her first husband through cancer while she was still young, and her present husband had been paralysed from head to toe for years. She was so devoted to him that she resisted every attempt by the hospital to make her hand him over to their care. And yet in spite of that, from her home she carried on an amazing work as the Area Secretary for LEPRA. Through this troubled time of change I could see Evelyn's spiritual life growing. She was clearly blossoming through the preaching and the worship. She would say quite definitely now, that her spiritual experience was revolutionized through the quiet work of the Holy Spirit that was going on. Evelyn's faith and enthusiasm were a tremendous support to us all—and especially to me.

As time went on, we were able to see that a spiritual reason lay at the heart of the objections. This is not to brand any of our folk as ungodly—indeed not, all were acting from worthy motives. But it was an undeniable fact that none of those who raised objections ever attended our prayer meetings or meetings designed to consider the future of the church. Although some were prominent in other ways in church life, it was indicative that when it came to the spiritual side of our life together, those who resisted change were not to be found among those waiting upon God and seeking his will.

Over the next two years as the church went through a remarkable period of change, some of those who were most unhappy left and went elsewhere. This was of deep personal regret because no pastor wants to drive people away. I visited each person individually to explain the church's policy on worship, but to no avail. But considering the turmoil of those months, with much more change still to come, it was remarkable how few actually left. Some indeed came back into fellowship as God worked in power, whilst others who remained as an unhappy caucus in the church were caught up by new life sweeping through the fellowship and they abandoned their entrenched attitudes.

Looking back over that period it is difficult to say what I would have done if I had the chance to live it over again.

Perhaps the changes were too many and made too quickly. I am prepared to concede that my own enthusiasm for change may have been a little too breathtaking for some. Yet against that must be set the urgency of the task. The need was there for all to see. The church was losing people because of the character of its worship. The overwhelming desire of the congregation was for the changes to be made—and made quickly. If we had proceeded at the speed of the slowest member of the caravan in order to maintain the congregation's unity, we might still be discussing worship now!

So the heart-searching went on alongside a quiet conviction that we were following God's will. The lesson God was trying to teach us was that faith—to be true faith—always contains an element of risk. There is the possibility, remote or otherwise, that one may be making a mistake. Faith is not travelling by sight, but on the basis of God's faithfulness to his people. If it is foolish to launch out in faith, then God's fool is one who is prepared to leave the safe and certain for the unmapped territory of the promised land. Signposts that we are travelling along the right road are the blessings that he gives us along the way. For us these blessings at that time were small ones, like the tangible signs of growth in the congregation, and a concern for our corporate prayer life.

There was, however, one glorious sign of the work God was longing to do, and that sign was Miriam, a young Jewish student. Miriam hadn't had much contact with Christians before coming to university, but when she arrived at St Mary's College she found a real love and acceptance from a group of Christian girls. She started to attend St Nic's and after a wavering start continued to come regularly. Then one day she invited Christ into her life and came to me wanting to be baptized. Of particular importance to her was the way our worship spoke to her life—another indication of the evangelistic potential of worship. Where worship is truly attractive and Christ-centred, it can be a powerful magnet for the gospel.

At her baptism, Miriam spoke simply and movingly about her faith in Jesus and what her faith meant to her. I was particularly struck by the emphasis she gave to worship and fellowship. 'Coming to church is of major importance to me now,' she said, 'Not only do I feel the love and acceptance of the congregation, but the worship moves me to offer to God my love, joy and all my being.'

Miriam was our first real conversion. Coming as it did in the context of all the battles over worship, in this event we saw her as a harbinger of the blessings to come. We wanted our church to touch the lives of many people like Miriam, and we lived in expectancy.

4

Song and Dance

In February 1976 David Watson, a well known British evangelist and leader within the renewal movement (known as the charismatic renewal), was in Durham leading the university mission. I took the opportunity to meet David, not for the first time, and to talk with him about St Nicholas's Church. We had lunch together, and I described our situation, including the opportunities and difficulties. David was as usual very discerning in his observations. 'Clarify the vision,' he said, 'Make sure that what you want to achieve are God's objectives and not your own fancies. A Spirit-filled church is not built overnight. It comes as a result of a spiritual, praying congregation who are prepared to go all the way with God.'

That meeting helped me to sort out my thinking concerning the charismatic movement. I had long felt ambivalent about this movement which had swept through all the mainstream denominations. My own experience of renewal had taught me to affirm and accept all that it said about the gifts and graces of the Spirit being available to God's people. I too was convinced that the church needed to rediscover all that the New Testament showed to be the inheritance of Christians.

But on the other hand I had never been a terribly strong

party man. Although I had become a Christian through the evangelical wing of the church and identified with it theologically, I preferred to be free and open to embrace God's truth from whatever part of the Christian fold it came. I felt similarly about the charismatic movement. It spoke to my heart and I agreed to most of its teaching, but somehow in my bones I knew that I could not be a 'paid-up' member of this movement either.

There was one major theological difference between my approach and that of many within the charismatic movement—I could not see any scriptural evidence for a 'baptism' of the Holy Spirit if this meant that all Christians were called to enter a second stage of spiritual initiation. Such a rigid differentiation I could not accept, even though I agreed absolutely with my friends at the centre of the movement that God wanted to pour out his Spirit on all flesh, and that the gifts of the Holy Spirit are there to be claimed and used in his service. Instead of the term 'baptism of the Spirit' I prefer to use such terms as 'fullness' of the Spirit, or 'release' of the Spirit, because it appears self-evident to me that there is not such a being as a Spirit-less Christian. There are plenty of disobedient Christians around who refuse to allow the Holy Spirit to have his sovereign way in their lives, but there cannot be Christians unbaptized in the Holy Spirit. Impoverished and stunted they may be, but not without the Spirit of God.

Although I had cause to be deeply grateful for all I had learned through the renewal movement, I felt that we had to find our own way forward. We too could learn from this contemporary movement of the Spirit, but it was wrong just to ape what was going on elsewhere in more successful churches. We could not be sure where the Spirit wanted to take us or what he wanted to do with us—all I was sure about was that we had to be open to him.

But the music and songs of the renewal movement

influenced us very profoundly and made us more open to the Spirit's work. Veronica and a few others were still bravely leading the group, but it was quite obvious that we needed a particularly rare person to take over the music of the church and lead it on to new possibilities. Someone who was not only an able musician but also someone who shared my own convictions concerning renewal. God supplied that person in an unusual way. Dr Ron Hancock, a GP in North London phoned one day: 'My son Christopher and his wife Suzie are moving to Durham. Chris is going to train for the ministry at Cranmer Hall. They can't move into their home for a few weeks. Have you any suggestions where they might store their furniture?' 'Surely,' I said. 'What about our upper church hall? It is rarely used. They can use that until their home is ready.'

When Chris and Suzie arrived with the van and started to unload their furniture, I noticed the careful way Chris was handling a cello. 'Are you a musician?' I asked, getting very interested as an idea started to form in my head. 'Well, of sorts,' replied Chris laughing. As we talked about church music and as Chris shared with me his philosophy, I got more and more excited. Surely this is God's man, I thought!

For some weeks, Chris and Suzie were undecided about their church commitment. We were still going through major disputes concerning worship and that kind of turbulence is enough to put anyone off going into the firing line. But eventually Chris took over the leadership of the music group, and it began to blossom. This was simply due to Chris's conviction, shared and backed by myself, that the group had to be open to renewal itself before it could be a channel of change. 'A music group is first and foremost a prayer group and only secondly a music group,' he would repeat. And it is probably true that for the first year of Chris's year of office more time was spent by the group in sharing and praying than in actual music practice.

At first some of the group complained about the amount of time spent on waiting upon God. 'I came along to sing—not to pray,' said one girl. Chris's reply was firm and courteous: 'If you just want to sing, then go along to the Choral Society. But if you want to make an effective contribution to the music group you must learn that our role is central to the Church's worship. We must be sensitive to the Spirit before we can be used by the Spirit.'

This emphasis upon the group as a spiritual entity made an instant impact, not only upon individuals in the music group, but upon the congregation as well.

First, it led to an awareness in the music group that those engaged in any aspect of leadership in the church had to be open to God. And a quiet but important ministry started in the group. As they learned to share spiritual experiences, and prayed and worked together, so the Holy Spirit led them into fresh experiences of his life and power. Some felt a deeper longing to enter more fully into the life of the Spirit. Through the laying on of hands they were filled afresh with the Spirit's presence. One girl who suffered from depression was healed through the support and prayer of the group. A number received the gift of tongues which revolutionized their own spiritual lives, increasing their own sense of devotion to the Lord as well as their effectiveness in intercession.

But this also led to a deepening appreciation within the congregation of the importance and power of music. Organ, electric piano, flute and guitars, led by the rich tones of Chris's cello, gave a depth to our singing that was gladly received by the vast majority. It is certainly true that when the Spirit moves in a congregation, joy and praise are dominant notes in the Spirit's orchestration. Augustine once wrote, 'He who praises prays twice,' and the sound of praise to our triumphant God, according to that arithmetic, clearly denoted a lot of praying going on!

It is also a fact noted in the history of revival and renewal that creativity in music is a side effect of any movement of the Spirit. From the music group and also from within the congregation, new songs began to appear. One girl in the music group going through a time of deep spiritual anguish was encouraged by the rest of the group to bring out her faith and her search in a song. The beautiful song she wrote catches the mixture of sadness and faith:

> O Jesus, you are truly wonderful,
> And Jesus, is it really true
> That all men who believe in you,
> The only Son of God,
> Shall find redemption
> Through your blood?

I have often been asked if it is right for a Christian song to express that kind of spiritual crisis, and I have always answered that indeed it is, as long as faith is the dominant note. Too many songs give the impression that the Christian life is easy and that the power of the Holy Spirit is as instantly available as switching on a light switch. Too few express the kind of heart searching and questioning which that girl went through. That song became one of our most popular songs—perhaps because it combined that element of faith and questioning which is at the heart of normal human experience.

The success of the music group eventually led us to make a major change in our worship pattern. For a long time I had been unhappy by the minor role given to Holy Communion services in the church. As in most evangelical churches we had Holy Communion twice a month—once in the morning and once in the evening. At other times a shortened form of the Holy Communion service was tagged onto an abbreviated form of morning or evening prayer. This was clearly unsatisfactory because as well as declaring implicitly that we did not regard Holy Communion as important, it meant that the congregation did not meet frequently around the Lord's table.

'Besides,' went an argument, 'if we had more Holy Communion services, we would find it more difficult to reach the outsider. Holy Communion is for Christians only, and more frequent Communion will drive uncommitted people away.'

Yet, it was clear that now we had introduced a sung setting of the Communion service, led so beautifully by the music group, our Holy Communion services were more popular than any other service! A questionnaire showed that the majority of the congregation were in favour of more frequent Communions, and we took the important decision to make Holy Communion our central service each Sunday, alternating it morning and evening, so as to give both congregations a chance to take part in it more often. Far from the Holy Communion being a major obstacle to the outsider, we discovered that its stress upon the death and resurrection of Jesus is a powerful evangelistic image. When this is connected with lively, reverent worship, it can be an attractive force for the kingdom of God.

This major change in our worship pattern was probably the most important single step in our time at St Nicholas's. Not only did it lead the congregation into a discovery of the importance of the sacramental in the Christian life, it also made it possible for Christians of other traditions to join us in fellowship. The Holy Communion became a uniting and healing bridge.

My part-time colleague Graeme Rutherford was unconvinced and a bit worried by these developments. Graeme, a young Australian doing a post-graduate degree in Theology, had been brought up in the Reformed tradition. He had a high doctrine of Scripture and a great love for the pulpit. 'I'm worried that we may be in danger of undermining the evangelical tradition of St Nic's,' he declared. 'An emphasis upon a weekly Communion service is sure to detract from the preaching of the word. Let's go more slowly!' Graeme's worries were unfounded because we had no intention of cutting on the teaching ministry of the church. But it was a viewpoint shared by some, and it was clear that the ministry of preaching should not be a casualty of change.

But if the music group was an issue of some magnitude, the dance group was to be even more so! A number of us were convinced that liturgical dance, as it is sometimes called, has a place in worship. It is often referred to in the Old Testament, and there is ample evidence of dance and movement used as expressions of worship in the early and medieval church. Unfortunately, one of the regrettable side effects of the Reformation was the passive role given to worshippers whose main duty appeared to be to hear the word expounded. Our bodies were ignored as if they have no place within Christian spirituality.

Around springtime 1976, a young lady by the name of Chris Ledger was having coffee with Eileen in the vicarage. Chris and her husband John had recently moved to Durham. I had just begun to ask Chris what she had done in the past. 'Before I went into nursing,' she said, 'I had professional dance training, but...' 'Why, that's tremendous,' I said excitedly; 'have you ever considered using your gift of dance in worship?' 'Go on!' cried Chris bursting into laughter, 'You can't use dance in Christian worship!' The peals of laughter rang around the kitchen. Later, Chris told me that she was thinking at the time, 'Funny, why get so excited about dance? What a strange vicar!' We had a long discussion about dance as a medium of communication, and Chris promised to go away and consider it more carefully, taking away with her a few books on the subject.

Very soon, a group of young ladies began to meet regularly to explore dance as an element of worship. As with the music group the dance group was primarily a praying, spiritual fellowship. Indeed, many of us would go so far as to say that its commitment to prayer and renewal was at the heart of the renewal of the church as a body.

The first dance by the group was in the autumn of 1976 when in the context of worship they danced to the hymn *Holy, Holy, Holy, Lord God Almighty*. It was a beautiful expression of love to God, and it was appreciated by most of the congregation because it was performed with great finesse, each movement subordinate to the words which it was attempting to interpret.

Of course, dance coming at the very point when grievances over worship were coming to the boil just added fuel to the fire! Fortunately, the fact that Eileen was in the dance group added a touch of respectability to it—if the Vicar's wife is in it, it must be all right! But that did not stop dance becoming one of the major points of tension. Chris, as leader, experienced a little of the unpleasantness when a lady in the congregation refused to speak to her because of her position.

Why was it, a number of us wondered, that dance attracted such hostility? It wasn't as if we overused it in worship; nor was it possible to confuse this style of expression with flimsily clad young ladies cavorting on our television screens! There were three possible reasons why dance is often a focal point of criticism.

First, you can't avoid the visual impact of dance, short of closing your eyes. It is a direct bridge with the meaning of a song or hymn. It can challenge a person in a way that few other forms of expression can because it makes emotion physical. You can express joy, sadness, praise and other emotions in movement and they can be brought embarrassingly close to people—sometimes too close for comfort. Whereas in other forms of communication, such as preaching or singing, emotion may be kept at arm's length or privatized.

Secondly, dance breaks with the traditional passive role given to worshippers in a church service. The order of the liturgy, the normality of Anglican worship, is suddenly interrupted by a group of lay people arising from the congregation to express their faith in dance. Because it is unfamiliar, it is likely to be questioned and attacked. We learned from experience that it was unfair on the congregation to be suddenly confronted with a dance. They need to be prepared psychologically for something that lies outside normal experience. We also discovered that it helps the congregation to receive a dance if someone introduces it carefully.

Thirdly, because it is an interpretative medium, dance is not explicit. It cannot express absolutely what it is symbolizing. The task of interpretation has to be worked at by both dancers and congregation alike. The dancers have to develop skills beyond the amateurish arm waving and pirouetting. If it is offered to God only the best will do in the long run. The congregation also must be taught to appreciate dance as a Christian art-form. Men particularly—and evangelical men more than most—have difficulty in seeing the point of dance, because their natural inclination is to bypass as forms of worship movement, colour, beauty and indeed most forms of the symbolic, except the verbal.

But there was one important area where the dance group helped the congregation to break through a very important cultural barrier—that of a rather middle-class attitude to any form of spontaneity, or overt expressions of praise. As a young working-class Christian I used to wonder from my experience of going to football matches why it was that enthusiasm was frowned upon in church worship. Go to any decent football ground and you will experience enthusiasm expressed in singing, arm waving, cheering and so on. If our faith is important to us, I used to muse, why shouldn't we too be moved to express our faith in ways that are true to us as individuals? Instead we sing glorious hymns like *Praise My Soul the King of Heaven* as if we are paying the milk bill; or, if we are Anglicans, we sing the *Te Deum* 'We praise you, O Lord, we acknowledge you to be the Lord' (originally intended as a triumphant anthem against the opposition of all who reject Christ) as if we are taking a dose of cod liver oil!

The dance and music groups helped us to be a little more free in our worship, to raise our arms in praise (if we wanted to) or to clap during the singing of choruses. This did not go on, by any means, during every hymn or chorus. It would not have been natural or spontaneous if individuals felt the pressure of the group to respond in only one way. But dance especially had an important part in helping to create a more 'released' congregation.

One person who found dance difficult to come to terms with was Caroline Rutherford, wife of my colleague. If Graeme was concerned about the gentle drift of the church towards renewal, Caroline found that dance threatened her in an indefinable way. To make matters worse, Caroline had been asked by the dance group to play the piano for them on their practice evenings! While she was willing to help them out, she admitted that she found their times of sharing together difficult.

And yet a surprising and wonderful thing was to happen to Graeme and Caroline. In 1977 they returned to Australia, and Graeme was appointed Rector of Kyabram in the Melbourne Diocese. Kyabram Parish Church was a fellowship of great potential, and Graeme and Caroline went there with great enthusiasm and with no lack of ideas. But their ministry met with little success, and they were forced to question their assumptions. Eventually they were led to throw themselves onto the resources of

God and to seek his way for their ministry. While they were at this point of human despair they were invited to a charismatic renewal service at a nearby Roman Catholic Church. At the end of the service, Graeme and Caroline received the laying on of hands and were led into a deeper experience of the Holy Spirit and his power.

Considering Graeme's former Reformed views this seems, as in my case too, a little like one of God's jokes. But Graeme and Caroline's willingness to allow the Holy Spirit total control resulted in a revolution in their ministry and the most exciting developments in their church life. We at St Nic's, hearing what had happened to this couple, saw this as a thrilling example of what God can do. He is the God of the unexpected, and no one is beyond his power to renew. Graeme and Caroline's situation seemed to say, 'The only precondition to the renewal of faith is surrender.' And we longed to see our church community really surrendered to God's will and totally committed to him.

We knew we had a long way to go.

5

Build My Church

It is a fact that many of mankind's achievements have resulted from accident or good fortune. I love the story of the discovery of the electric motor. At the Vienna exhibition of 1873, a machine attendant by chance connected two cables to a dynamo that was standing idle. To everyone's great surprise the armature of the dynamo commenced to revolve at great speed. It was found that the two cables led to another dynamo that was running at the time and the current supplied by it had converted the stationary dynamo into an electric motor. I don't suppose that anyone knows the name of that man. And it is very possible that he did not get any credit for discovering a source of power which is at the heart of modern civilization.

It was a similar curious course of events that led us into making a revolutionary breakthrough, though here we may say 'chance' had very little to do with it! In June 1976, a number of us met to discuss the mission of the church and how we might be more effective. I remember our first meeting very well. We met in the vicarage after the evening service. It was a lovely clear evening. We spent a considerable time praying about the work of the church and how we might become a more effective Christian community. We discussed the usual things—guest services, missions, parish visitation, and so on. The assumption behind our thinking was, 'Let's go out and evangelize them. Let's bring them into our fellowship.' This is not necessarily wrong, but in our context we failed to look at ourselves. We didn't stop to ask, 'Is there anything attractive about us that might draw others in?'

One of the members of the group was Brenda Blake. Brenda went home and shared our discussion with her husband Gerald, and it was, to use the analogy of the electric motor, as if we had connected two dynamos together.

Gerald phoned me that evening. 'George, Brenda has shared with me the ideas of the evangelistic group. I think I have something which bears on this. If it is not too presumptuous to say, I think I have glimpsed a vision of what God wants us to do.'

The following afternoon, Gerald and I met. 'The other day,' said Gerald, 'I walked into the church and looked around. It was a beautiful afternoon, but the sun seemed to show up all the defects of the building. I looked at the crumbling masonry, the creaking, battered and uncomfortable pews, the cobwebs and dust out of reach of the cleaner, the cold, forbidding and inflexible interior—I wondered how we have the nerve to invite anyone to church. Frankly, I'm ashamed to invite anyone!'

'I'm inclined to agree with you,' I replied. 'The church is showing signs of coming alive and we are beginning to realize that the buildings are hopelessly inadequate for our work. What can we do?'

'Well,' said Gerald excitedly, 'I have taken the liberty of putting down on paper a project for a two-year programme of modernization and development. Here it is. What do you think?'

Gerald's vision was an amazing restructuring of the church. He saw the church at the heart of the city as an open, attractive building, properly furnished, decorated and equipped. A centre where there would be activity seven days a week. He saw it offering hospitality and social care; a place, in fact, that would be a natural bridge between the Christian church and the outside world.

As I read over Gerald's plans I began to share his excitement. It was as if God had given us the key to an exciting future. Of course! Where we had gone wrong was in assuming that we were like any other ordinary church ministering to a Sunday morning congregation. While this was important, our situation was different from many other churches. We were the Market Square Church. Thousands passed our doors every day. Our ministry was there in the Market Place. It was surely right to make the building a place that proclaimed, 'Our God is alive!'

A week passed, and I convened a meeting so that David Gregory-Smith and Gerald Brooke, our church wardens, could meet Gerald and myself to discuss the matter further. Gerald shared his scheme with typical enthusiasm and charm. 'Why,' he said, 'we could complete this by April 1978, and it would only cost £50,000 or so!'

Both church wardens were wonderful Christian leaders of faith and vision. But as we talked together the cold wind of realism tempered the hot air of enthusiasm. Gerald Brooke, a practical Christian man, asked some necessary but uncomfortable questions. 'Yes, I agree,' he said, 'it is a marvellous idea, but our track record is not very good. We are talking about changes that will cost the earth. Two years ago we were rejoicing when the church raised £140 on a Gift Day. Where is the money going to come from? It's all very well saying that God will provide. I believe that. But his people do not appear to share his spirit of generosity!' Gerald was so right. The church's performance to date did not inspire any confidence that it would respond to a radical plan of development.

'On the other hand,' said David, the other warden, 'if

this is God's will for the church, then we must assume that he will provide and equip us.' We agreed that the next step was for this scheme to be shared with the Church Council. If they did not believe that it was right, then it would have to be abandoned.

To our joy, the Council by an overwhelming majority agreed that the scheme ought to be considered very carefully. One of the first things we did was to set aside a day of prayer for people to pop into the church and pray for the church and its ministry as well as wider concerns. I was dreadfully disappointed by the turnout. I remember reflecting, how could we possibly ask for God's blessing on such a radical undertaking when only forty or so people turned out to pray? What commitment did it indicate? Were we ready to tackle such a scheme?

Ready or not, it was as if we had switched on a current which now energized the whole church. A number of us drew up mini-papers which looked at our ministry, worship and evangelism. A special meeting was called to acquaint the congregation with the proposals, and a Steering Committee was created to advise the Council, and finally a well known British architect, Ronald Sims of York, was appointed to work alongside the Steering Committee.

The Steering Committee's ideas gradually took shape. We wanted seating for more than the present number of 400; we wanted a large carpeted area with stackable chairs for worship, concerts, lectures, films and festivals; and we wanted halls for smaller gatherings, a good historical display, an information centre, a bookstall, a welcome area, counselling rooms and decent toilet facilities.

Soon news leaked out to the wider community and I hit the headlines. 'Vicar wants Rock Groups in Church!' 'Out goes the old—in comes the new!' '"Sacrilege!" says old resident!' All of it was complete rot, but it is completely true that when God moves a congregation the devil hits back. And often he uses the well meaning intentions of decent people to block the way of the Spirit. We found that objections came from some members of the congregation who began to show an unnatural commitment to special parts of the church's interior—the pews, the organ, the children's corner, and so on. From outside the church, people complained that they did not want changes to the church they were married in—even though they had not been back since!

If I had not been convinced already that a radical plan was necessary, I would have been by two events that followed. The first was a wedding at the church. On that occasion I was present as a guest and someone else was conducting the wedding. It was a very cold, wet day, and I got a distinctly chilly 'pew perspective' on the church. To my great horror, water was flooding through the roof and dropping onto the pew in front. What a dreadful witness for the Christian faith, I thought. At the reception after I overheard a man saying, 'I've never been so cold in all my life. I'm glad I don't have to return to that church in a hurry!' This reinforced my thinking that the church building was a major stumbling block to the gospel. The coldness, dampness, dreariness and inflexibility of the building all conspired to make it a poor vehicle for communicating the Christian faith.

The next prod from the Lord that radical changes were needed came when I had a visit from Ken who was the secretary for Age Concern in Durham. Ken saw the strategic position of the church—its proximity to the Post Office, bus stops and shops—and he came to share a problem with me.

'We have a terrible problem of loneliness among elderly people in Durham. We at Age Concern are very worried about it, and we would like to set up a drop-in centre for elderly folk.' I was interested to hear Ken's views because they overlapped with mine. I saw a need for a drop-in centre, although I was concerned also about the homeless and the aimless youngsters who drifted about.

Ken continued to talk about his proposal. 'What we would like to do is to combine our resources with yours and perhaps use your hall for a drop-in centre. Are you interested?' I told Ken we were very interested, and I invited him to look over our facilities. Half an hour later, Ken returned shifting uncomfortably and looking embarrassed. 'I'm sorry, but I had no idea that the buildings were so, well... so uncomfortable and cold. They are just not suitable for old people, and I'm afraid there is no way we can use them. Sorry about that!'

Eventually our architect, Ronald Sims, produced his solution to our needs. And how revolutionary they were! As we saw his plans our excitement rose. He had swung the focal point of the church so that the holy table was in the middle; his plans included narrow galleries running alongside the north and south walls; he had included extra rooms because of the extra floors; there was a pyramid-like false ceiling. There was much besides—but his plans indicated that he could make of this drab Victorian building a place of beauty and service, such as it never was before. He estimated that the cost would be about £220,000—not Gerald's guess of £50,000! Could the church take on board such a radical and expensive plan?

We on the Steering Committee felt dazed, daunted and yet very excited—but how would the whole church family feel? Was this of the Lord? Very soon we would know the answer.

While all the talking, praying and business about the building was going on, there were a number of ways in which God manifested his presence among us and confirmed that he was very much around.

The first way was how he brought together the leadership which made the whole project possible. Richard Briggs played a central role in our planning. Richard, however, was not a practising Christian when our planning started. When I visited his wife, Elizabeth, a member of our Church Council, I discovered that Richard rarely came to church. He explained that church made him feel claustrophobic and there was no doubt that this was a serious problem to him. I found out that Richard was a senior Planning Officer. Just the chap to help us with our plans for redevelopment! And Richard agreed to join in the Steering Committee. And as he got more and more involved, so his spiritual life began to blossom, because we made no secret of the spiritual basis of our scheme. At every Steering Committee there was much prayer and our desire to service Christ was uppermost. In a quiet but gentle way Richard entered upon the Christian life and went on from strength to strength.

I will never forget the Sunday afternoon Richard came to see me and we talked over his spiritual pilgrimage. Later we prayed together and Richard uttered his first prayer aloud. Humanly speaking, without Richard we would have found the going very tough indeed, but God gave him to us as he did every member of that leadership team. A young Christian, he was having an amazing ministry among the fellowship.

Another touch of God's gracious concern was about my role. For the first eighteen months of my ministry at St Nic's it was largely a one-man-band, in spite of the lay support and activity. I had no secretarial help, no full time curate, no typewriter, no duplicator—no office, in fact. I did, however, have the assistance of two honorary curates, and they were invaluable. With the advent of the building project more work came my way and the strain was beginning to show.

I remember one Saturday evening in particular when I was in my study faced with a sermon to complete and the whole magazine to duplicate and put together for the morning. I could see disaster looming ahead and my frustration boiled over. 'Look, Lord,' I exploded, 'look at what I've got to do before tomorrow—a sermon and the whole magazine.' And like the psalmist I ranted on at God. And then it suddenly dawned on me: 'Whose work is it anyway? If it is God's work—why should I do God's worrying for him?' And so I prayed aloud: 'Lord, here I am, your servant, worrying about your work, assuming that you don't care and are not involved. Lord, help me to do my serving joyfully and well.'

It was a mental transaction. I handed back to the Lord his work and the lovely thing was, the weight was lifted from my shoulders and each and every job got done! Very shortly after, a young lady in the congregation became the part-time church secretary and I was a beast of burden no more!

The second way we saw God preparing the ground for our developing ministry was that he made it possible for us to have a curate. It happened in an amazing way. I had been told by the Bishop that in spite of the many activities the church had, the size of the parish did not warrant a curate. But early in April 1977, just before Easter on a Friday afternoon, I had the uncanny feeling that I ought to phone the Bishop of Jarrow about the matter. He listened to my request and said, 'I'm sorry, George, the verdict stands. We shall be discussing the allocation of staff at the Diocesan Staff Meeting on Monday. But there will be no change of policy.' My heart sank, but I urged him to consider our application in the light of all that was happening. He agreed to bear this in mind, and we hung up.

The following Monday I had to go to London, and on the platform I met the Archdeacon of West Auckland. To my joy, he told me that at Friday staff meeting the Diocese agreed to let me have a curate—'if you can get one at this late stage.' Bubbling over with delight I attended my meeting in London and to my surprise found myself sitting next to the Principal of St John's Theological College,

Nottingham. I passed to him a note: 'Robin, have you any chaps looking for a curacy—or am I too late?' Back came the scribbled note: 'One left. Pete Broadbent. Interested?'

Were we interested! A number of us in the church knew Pete and Sarah to be outstanding people. It was almost as if God had been saving them for us.

But what about accommodation? We had none. However, the series of surprising events continued—the person who defined miracles as 'God's coincidences' could have been writing for our situation. I returned from that meeting in London to find that I had to take a funeral two days later. I visited the home, found that the son wished to sell the house, and with the Church Council's speedy blessing we put down the deposit. The house was three doors away from the Youth Centre—exactly where we needed a staff house! By Easter Monday, Pete and Sarah visited the church and agreed to come. Within the space of seven days this sequence of events had taken place: the sudden urge to phone the Bishop, Diocesan go-ahead given on a railway platform, sitting next to the College Principal, the availability of Pete and Sarah, the availability of the house next to the Youth Centre, the vision of the PCC to respond. If that isn't miraculous, I don't know what is!

The arrival of Pete and Sarah was to be another significant step forward, because both brought strong gifts to share. As individuals and as a community we were beginning to see God's faithfulness exercised among us in all kinds of ways. It is not surprising that one of our favourite hymns as we responded to his goodness was:

Great is thy faithfulness, O God my Father,
There is no shadow of turning with thee.

6

Renew My People

'More and more churches will have to do what you are doing. It's bad economics and probably bad Christianity for churches to be open and heated for just one day a week.' Colonel Miller voiced his approval of our plans for major redevelopment. As Chief Executive of Durham, he was very much in favour of progress. 'Keep it up, Padre, and if the City Council can help, just call on us.'

By now, practically everyone in Durham knew about our plans, although some wild ideas were going round. One story that came back to me was that the church was going to be changed into a dance-hall! I was quite happy for people to dance for the Lord, but even I would draw a line at a quick-step on Sunday morning! Putting aside such ludicrous notions, what thrilled the leadership of St Nic's was the support we were getting from so many outside the narrow fellowship of the church. We had contacted the diocese, the cathedral staff and other churches, and all were very encouraging. And now our friends in the Town Hall were voicing their approval too.

But the people who really mattered were the congregation. Without its wholehearted commitment to the project in prayer, energy and money, we could not go forward.

It was vital, therefore, to prepare the congregation for the momentous decision. After receiving the architect's drawings, we decided to spend the whole of the summer and autumn of 1977 involving the congregation in discussing the ministry of the church in the light of the plans.

Our first congregational meeting in early July was an unforgettable affair. After a congregational lunch we crammed together in the dingy upper hall. I had already decided that it would help to make the meeting more open and natural if I did not chair the meeting, so Peter Green, lay chairman of the church, took the chair.

After outlining the plans briefly, Peter invited contributions from those present. A few voices spoke warmly of the need for main change. But then very quickly the dominant mood changed from enthusiasm to anxiety and opposition. 'We are talking about hundreds of thousands of pounds!' 'Should we be spending such a large sum on ourselves when thousands are dying from hunger abroad?' asked another.

These were natural questions and attempts were made to respond to them. First, that God could provide, but the project did demand a level of commitment such as we had never given before. And secondly, the project flowed from a deep missionary concern for the church's ministry in Durham. If it was genuinely of God it should lead to a deeper commitment to the overseas church.

But suddenly a person who had opposed the changes in worship stated, 'The whole thing is ridiculous! You say that there is a real need for such a programme of modernization. I am not convinced. You talk of the church being opened and manned seven days a week—bookstalls, coffee and meals being served—and we have difficulties finding people willing to be Sunday School teachers. Quite frankly the scheme is idiotic!'

Deathly silence followed the outburst. Then other

people chipped in to voice their support of the speaker. Was there a real need to change the church so radically? Of course improvements to the toilets, halls and kitchens were greatly needed—but was it necessary to do any more?

And then the pendulum swung back the other way as others spoke of their conviction that, if we looked at the church from our angle as Sunday worshippers, it was probably a valid point of view to leave the building as it was. But is the church only for Christians? Haven't we a duty to reach out to care, love and show the relevance of Christianity? And testimony flowed as some present shared their faith in Christ and their desire for the church to be an open, caring fellowship.

Following this introductory meeting, a number of house groups were organized over the summer so that every member of the congregation knew what was going on and had a chance to air his views.

It was at this point that Richard Briggs and I made an interesting and sobering discovery. It was difficult to gauge the real strength of the congregation. The presence of students and visitors often gave the impression that we were a large congregation. Although we had grown, we had no accurate idea of our membership, so Richard and I went over the membership list of the church and found that our local congregation was only about 130 strong. This was an important find because it pin-pointed two things clearly—that it would be foolish to overestimate the resources of the congregation, and if we did not have complete confidence in God's power, we might as well scrap the project at once.

Over that summer about 150 people met in house groups to talk about and to pray for the proposed Building Project. They were asked to consider the ministry of the church and if the architect's plans really expressed God's will for us, as far as we could test it. As summer passed into autumn, the reports coming in from the house groups were positive and encouraging. It was clear that the congregation as a whole was responding magnificently to the task of seeking God's will. Although there were some who had major misgivings about the scheme, most were convinced that something had to be done—God's mission was hindered by the building we had.

October arrived, and the Church Council met to discuss and decide on the Building Project. Excitement mounted in the congregation, with not a little fear and hesitation. The consequences following agreement to go forward were immense. We recognized that if that were the case, it would be like the Israelites crossing the Red Sea—a step of faith into a level of commitment never entered before. And, on the other hand, what if the Council said no? A number thought that to pull back now and retreat from such an exciting adventure, in which many of us recognized the hand of God, would be a serious act of faithlessness.

The Council met in the vicarage as normal, but there was an abnormal atmosphere surrounding our meeting on this occasion. Usually there would be a light-hearted spirit, a relaxed atmosphere of Christian fellowship and bonhomie—but on this occasion we were tense and concerned: the moment of decision had arrived.

The Steering Committee presented its recommendation—that it firmly believed that the church's ministry was seriously hindered by the shoddy facilities, and recommended that the Church Council commit itself to the project.

Peter Green in measured tones conveyed the urgent need for improvement; 'The roof, the walls and the interior require immediate attention. If we put it off we shall only have to consider it another time!'

'But need it be so drastic?' asked someone, worried by the enormous sum of money mentioned. 'Why don't we just do up the areas that need attention and leave the rest until we can afford it?'

'It's not a question of what we can afford,' said Alison Foote, a young teacher. 'Surely it is a matter of following God's will. Our attention should not be on repairing a building, but renewing its ministry.'

'That's right,' chipped in John Ledger, another member of the Steering Committee. 'The present building is a stumbling block to the gospel because it confirms the man in the street's worst impressions of the church as a dying institution. At the moment we cannot use it for any other purpose than church services.'

Dick Bongard, a former church warden, bravely voiced the hesitations of the older members of the congregation. 'No one denies that improvements are needed, but many of the changes are not accepted by older members. Why can't we go ahead to improve what the majority of the congregation can accept—for example the kitchen and halls?'

It was well after ten o'clock when the decision was made. It had become plain after the long discussion that we were not united, and a tired and subdued Church Council made its decision—that 'they could not in principle accept the plans'. However, the Council committed itself to rededicating the church to the Lord's service and to seek to develop its ministry and modernize the building. Minor improvements were accepted to satisfy the majority of the congregation.

It was a devastating climax to a period of intense heart-searching and prayer. Many believed that the Holy Spirit was calling us through the project to a new era in the church's life. And the Council's decision seemed to be a shocking betrayal of the promise. The Steering Committee were particularly downcast. Gerald Blake's reaction was a mixture of desolation and trust: 'My initial reaction was that of anger—how could the Council be so blind! And then I thought, "We know we are called to do something radical. We will be proved right in the end.'''

My own reaction was mixed also. I shared the feeling of bitter disappointment. And yet now that the moment of truth had arrived it all seemed so obvious. The Council had made the correct decision because the church was not ready. The Steering Committee's recommendation was quite right—but we had failed to realize that before we could use a renewed building we had to be a renewed people. Our disunity over the project, our fear of the problem of raising such a large sum of money, indicated an unrenewed congregation who had to be released by the Holy Spirit.

It was clear then that grievous as the Council's decision was, God was telling us something so clearly that we would have been spiritually stone-deaf to have misunderstood. He was saying: 'I am more interested in you than a fine building. Unless you are renewed, a lovely place is beside the point. When you are made alive then I will bring this thing to pass.'

7

The Spirit Moves

In my ministry I cannot claim to have had many direct
words from the Lord. Some Christians have the confidence
to say, 'The Lord gave me this verse.' This has not been
part of my normal experience, even though I am convinced
that God does speak clearly to his people. But following
the Council's decision not to go ahead with the project, a
passage of Scripture came to me with such force that I
knew that it was meant to be shared. And on the first
Sunday morning of January 1977, I preached on the
passage and emphasized that God wanted to pour out his
blessing on us. The passage was from Acts 4 and was the
story of the church in Jerusalem facing persecution. 'Don't
preach the name of Jesus—or else,' the apostles had been
threatened. Peter and John returned to the praying church
and they laid the problem before God. 'Sovereign Lord,
you hear the threats of these people ... but stretch forth
your hand to heal and minister in the name of Jesus.'
After they had prayed, the Holy Spirit fell on the congregation with the result that the passage concludes: 'with
great power the people testified to the resurrection of
Jesus, and great grace was upon them all.'

'I believe that God is calling us to reach out this year
into new areas of experience and ministry,' I said in my

sermon. 'Let us call upon his power, and, yes, let us even expect miracles! God is not dead—it is often our response and our faith that is dead. Let us have the same expectancy of the Holy Spirit as the church of Jerusalem had. Let us expect the Holy Spirit to renew us!'

As many of us realized by now, renewal of the people had to take place before we could return to the issue of the buildings. Our hearts had to be made ready and our lives shaped by the Spirit. But it was all very well having that as our goal—how were we going to achieve it?

First we felt that a precondition of renewal was an openness to God and a willingness to accept all that he wanted to do among us. At the heart of this is prayer. Not our usual form of 'lip service' to prayer, ritualized and church based—but the kind of praying based upon the conviction that the God of the Bible is active today. Modern secular living, which had weakened Christian belief in the power of God to work miracles, had to be challenged by bold believing prayer which 'expects the unexpected'. We had to become like the church in the United States which had the sign outside saying: 'Our God isn't dead, sorry about yours!' Our second aim was to have a regular praise and prayer evening which should have the highest profile in our life together. Our hope was that as we emphasized these two elements, the Holy Spirit would help us to respond to him and lead us into new experiences of his power.

One of my favourite sayings is, 'God never leaves identical fingerprints.' In other words, when he touches the lives of people he doesn't come with a rubber stamp, but he respects our individuality. Our response to him is therefore very different. Some come suddenly making a spectacular entrance into the kingdom of God, others come slowly and fearfully. Some have the experience of charismatic outpouring when they meet the Lord. Others do not.

A number of us in the leadership of the church felt very strongly that the unity of the Spirit could only be held if we respected the differences among us and accepted these differences as gifts for the body. It was certainly a mark of the Spirit's blessing that the wide variety of spiritual experiences was never divisive. There were those who were cautious of charismatic things and yet their lives were touched to go deeper into the things of the Spirit. Others, however, were definitely led into new experiences of the Holy Spirit, and we became used to talking freely about his gifts to us. As with many other evangelical churches we had grown used to reading about the experiences of the Spirit recorded in Scripture, but it hadn't dawned on us to ask if they applied to us today. Attempts to explain away the passages of the New Testament that talk about charismatic gifts by saying that they were for the New Testament period only are feeble and groundless excuses. Where does it say in Scripture that the gifts of the Spirit are only temporary? My own experience of the Spirit indicated we should take the New Testament evidence seriously if we wished to be the best for God.

And lovely signs of the Spirit's working emerged. We invited people to receive the laying on of hands for renewal in the Holy Spirit or for any personal need. In the Scripture the laying on of hands is a rite used for many different purposes—for healing, blessing, setting apart in ministry, ordination and infilling of the Spirit. We tried to make this as natural as possible in order to help people overcome fear and embarrassment. It was always a great joy to me personally when a Christian asked for prayer and the laying on of hands—not only because of the privilege to share with another Christian, but also as a thrilling experience to see another Christian encounter the goodness and faithfulness of God. One Thursday evening at our praise and prayer evening, two of the people present asked if we could pray for their friend who was to have a major operation the following day for the removal of a brain tumour. It was touch and go whether she would recover from the operation. We had a strong conviction that we should pray for complete healing for her. A few days later we learned that the operation had been successful and Judy was well on her way to full recovery. We were beginning to realize that God could be trusted with our problems and that he answered prayer.

But it wasn't all happening centrally. It was exciting to know that folk were meeting in two's and three's to pray together and share. As we began to talk more openly about these things there was a general relief that we were able to share such experiences together. One girl exclaimed, 'I used to think that I was the only one in the congregation who had had an experience of charismatic renewal. I was beginning to think I was the odd one out—now I find there are dozens like me!'

But as we observed earlier, it was not only by means of the overt signs of charismatic renewal that we were beginning to experience the presence of the Holy Spirit. The fruit of the Spirit was increasingly being manifested as our commitment to Jesus Christ deepened. 'By their fruits you shall know them,' said Jesus of the way that his followers may be known. The spiritual life declares itself in action.

One fruit of our spiritual response was the Friday lunches. The lunches were started to provide a contact with the outside community. Good meals were provided at modest prices. Alongside the lunch we usually presented a Christian activity either in the Market Square or in church. Gradually the lunches became very popular and drew into the church many people who would not otherwise pop in. For this activity we had to mobilize a large number from the congregation, because it just could not be done by three or four people. It was exciting to see ordinary Christians mingling with non-churchgoers, serving them and in some cases sharing their faith with them. One lady seeing the bustling activity, the banners dotting the church and noting the evident joy asked Elizabeth, one of our leaders, 'Is this a charismatic church?' Elizabeth, not too sure what answer to give, asked Eileen, 'Eileen, I have been asked if we are a charismatic church. Are we?' To which Eileen gave a splendid reply: 'If she means, "Are we copying what is going on elsewhere?" the answer is, "No, we are not." But if she means, "Are we open to the Spirit and what he wants to make us?" the answer is definitely, "Yes!"'

'Watersports' was another sign of the Spirit's movement among us. This activity was very largely the initiative of a retired gentleman, David White. David had been in the publishing business all his life. About five years before moving to Durham, he had lost his wife through cancer. His testimony of God was a moving and thrilling story. For most of his life he had been an atheist and very cynical of organized Christianity. But through his wife's illness and through his investigation into the claims of the Christian faith he was soundly converted. David was and is a wonderful example of a Christian who loves God and his fellow men wholeheartedly.

David popped in to see me one day to share his ideas about evangelism. 'You know I am keen on sailing,' he said. 'I have been giving some thoughts as to how I might turn this interest of mine into Christian service. It crossed my mind that it would be possible to take parties of people to the seaside and teach them to sail and canoe. As well as providing a worthwhile leisure activity we could share our faith in a relaxed and non threatening fashion.' This seemed to us all a marvellous idea and we gave David the freedom to develop his plan.

It was quite extraordinary how Watersports grew. From a tiny beginning with just one boat, David and his team were eventually running camps with five boats and twelve canoes. Most of us in the congregation were roped in to man the camps, give talks and cook. The activities included hill climbing and bird watching, as well as sailing and canoeing. It was indeed a great example of God using the skills of a retired gentleman who so easily could have said, 'Why bother to help others? It's my right to enjoy my retirement.' But David, with energy and enthusiasm, mobilized us all to make Watersports an enjoyable way of sharing the Christian faith. Not, mind you, in an aggressive way, but simply allowing the natural meeting point of having fun together to share our faith in Christ. God blessed these links with non-churchgoers and there was a steady trickle of people who found a living faith through Watersports.

Perhaps the most touching moments were when we took deprived children from Brandon Children's Home away with us. A number of us from the church had close links with this home for disturbed or maladjusted teen-agers, and each year a group of them would go on a Watersports holiday with us. For many of them it would have been their first holiday ever. It was a deeply humbling experience for those of us as leaders to witness the joy of such kids experiencing a holiday for the first time. Of course it was hardly a picnic for leaders—we had to recognize that things would be stolen and valuable property broken and fights would break out unexpectedly. These things we had to accept as part of the cost of sharing our faith.

'But Lord, we are conscious that we need very special gifts to reach out to the many people who pass the church every day.' As the Friday lunches developed and as our opportunities for sharing our faith grew, our prayer concern focused on the new ministries that were needed to capitalize on our unique situation. And God answered that prayer in a remarkable way when two final-year students made an appointment to see me.

They shuffled uncomfortably into my lounge and introduced themselves to me. I knew Mark Townson well as a regular student member of the congregation. But Alison Dumbell was new to me. They explained that they were members of a university Christian drama group known as The King's Men. 'We went on a mission quite recently,' said Alison, 'and we felt that God was calling us to offer our skills in his service.'

'What we would like to do,' continued Mark, 'is to base ourselves at St Nic's, but to be free to accept invitations up and down the country.'

'What about financial support?' I asked. 'Have you any guarantees for this ministry?'

'No,' they smiled, 'we just feel called at this moment to offer ourselves for his service. We are not asking St Nic's for money, but for prayer support. We are happy to live by faith. We believe that we can trust God for our needs.'

As I listened to their ideas of using their dramatic talents in God's service, I became quite convinced that Mark and Alison were God's answer to our need. 'I think this is a tremendous idea,' I replied, 'and I hope that our Church Council can do much more than just assure you of prayer support. I'll let you know what they have to say about it.'

Quite frankly, I never expected the Council to be as revolutionary as they were the night we discussed Mark and Alison. It had always been a thorough, painstaking body, considering items carefully and well. But that evening as we shared together Mark and Alison's vision for their ministry, an enthusiastic wave of support swept through the room.

'This is clearly of God,' argued Peter West, a recently appointed church warden. 'We must do more than just provide prayer support, important as this is. The least we can do is provide them with accommodation and pocket money.' Although this was a big undertaking for a small church, we agreed unanimously and decided to open a fund to be called the New Wine Fund. Bearing in mind that up to that time very few had seen Mark and Alison act together, it was a remarkable act of faith by the Council. Because they wanted to live by faith, we decided deliberately that the Fund would be administered separately by Richard Briggs, the church treasurer. We trusted the Lord to meet the needs of New Wine without having to support them from our general funds. The amazing thing was that, throughout the three-year period they worked with us, never once did the church have to supplement their ministry.

It was to be an exhilarating experience working so closely with them. They were two quite different people temperamentally as well as in terms of background. Alison was the daughter of probably the most prominent English fever specialist of the day. She was charming, sophisticated and middle class. Mark was working class, down to earth with a rough and ready approach. Alison was perhaps the better actor of the two, but Mark provided the ideas for the scripts and usually wrote them, so it was an ideal partnership.

The arrival of New Wine revolutionized our approach to reaching people with the message of Christ. They were willing to go anywhere and do anything. This meant that instead of waiting for people to come to a religious service before they could find out about the gospel, we could now go to them. Like the advert for a certain kind of lager which claims to reach the parts that other beers cannot reach—New Wine were able to go into situations that would otherwise be closed to more normal ways of expressing the Christian faith. Working Men's Clubs, the RAFA Club, the pubs and prisons of Durham were all in time to have New Wine presenting sketches. They were also very willing to do street theatre in Durham's busy Market Square, and large numbers were drawn to see and hear their presentation. As time went on they became more and more professional and expert, believing firmly that only the best for God would do.

A further way in which Mark and Alison made an impact upon us all was in their ability to illustrate sermon points for Pete and me. I well remember an example of this at Greenbelt when I was invited to give a talk about the Holy Spirit. I asked New Wine to come with me, to help me put across my material. Greenbelt is a well-known Christian music festival and I knew that I would have anything up to 700 people crowded into a marquee to hear this talk. I didn't want it to be a lecture, and I asked New Wine if they could help me put the teaching across dramatically. They came up with a tremendously funny sketch called 'Muscles Shrinking'. It was the story of a fighter who was a failure until he found a magic pair of boxing gloves, and it illustrated that the Christian life could only be lived in the power of the Spirit. It was sheer corn in terms of humour, but was a powerful way of putting a simple point across effectively.

Mark's own personal ministry was powerful in another way. He was very concerned about the plight of the Third World and that concern expressed itself in a radical life style. He ate very simply and his possessions were meagre to say the least. Just before his first Christmas with us he asked me if I would mind him erecting a shanty hut against the church wall in the Market Square.

'What on earth for, Mark?' I laughed. 'Have you been kicked out of your digs?' 'No, nothing like that,' replied Mark. 'What I want to do is to draw attention to two things. First that Christ was born in poverty and that millions live in squalor and hopelessness today. My idea is to collect rubbish—boxes, odd bits of wood and so on, and build a shanty hut. I will live in it for the week leading up to Christmas and live off boiled water and brown rice.'

A number of us were concerned about the effect this

might have upon Mark's health because it is one thing living like that in Calcutta, it's quite another thing living rough in Durham in the middle of winter.

But the idea was agreed and I got permission from the city authorities for Mark to build his shanty hut in a public place. And so a week before Christmas astonished shoppers found a shanty hut in the Market Place covered with Tear Fund posters depicting the needs of the Third World. It was a powerful and prophetic witness and it seared the consciences of many passers-by. Hundreds stopped to ask Mark what he was doing and it gave him a marvellous opportunity to talk simply about his Christian faith. He was able to say something about the meaning of Christmas as well as drawing attention to the plight of those in need. For three Christmases, Mark lived in his shanty hut and attracted wide publicity, extending even to radio and television. It showed the power of prophetic Christianity, especially when it proceeds from a genuine life style. Mark was conscious that he was being a fool for Christ's sake—but if we had more 'fools' like him the faith of Christ would truly flourish.

The year ended with a further sign of the Holy Spirit's blessing upon us. If God was going to renew his people it had to show in our willingness to be utterly available for his service. We decided to embark upon our own home-grown commitment campaign which we called 'Open to God'. Twenty or so of us began to meet from early September to plan and pray about the campaign. Each member of this team committed himself or herself to visit between six and ten people to talk about commitment to Christ. But before we could visit others we felt that we had to challenge one another. And this we did, exploring how much time we were giving to God's work and how we were using our skills and talents in his service. The question of money, which is usually seen as being at the very heart of normal stewardship campaigns, was deliberately put to one side. Not because money isn't important, but we were more concerned at this point that each member of the congregation should face up to the claims of Jesus and work them out fully, leaving the practical consequences to follow on.

As the team went out into the homes of the congregation, sermons on the theme of commitment were preached to help us work out how we were relating our faith in Christ to the way we lived. A report reached me that one infrequent member of the congregation had complained that we were always preaching about commitment. I was sad to hear this, because a church's teaching can become unbalanced and it is easy to preach commitment and neglect aspects like joy, peace and the freedom of the gospel. But as I went out of my way to teach, we can't know God's peace and power unless we know what Christian commitment is all about. If we want the best from God we must give him our best. As the reports from the visiting came in that autumn, we could see clear signs of a growing commitment to Christ and a willingness to work out the demands of Christian discipleship.

As the year ended I was surprised to realize that for almost a year we had totally put to one side discussion of the Building Project, which had so obsessed us the year before. So busy had we been urging a greater openness to the Holy Spirit that we had almost forgotten about it! And in small ways as well as big, God was at work in the congregation and the signs of his presence were beginning to show themselves. I was confident that if the church were truly open to God, it would eventually be open to the world.

8

Gifts for the Body

A mistake young Christians are apt to make is to assume that God only works through religious, churchy events. We locate him as expressing his life and power in particular ways, through stirring sermons, or in a moving Holy Communion service, or through healing services. We may have heard spellbound Christians say, 'When the Rev. Brown laid hands on people last night, over twenty people were healed! God was really present!' The implication being that when nothing happened last week God was having a day off! It is all too easy to restrict God to the God-slot and assume that 11:00 and 6:30 on Sundays are the divine times when God meets with his people.

As our congregation became more open to God, we began to learn that he works in the ordinary affairs of life. The theological way of putting this is to talk about the sacramentality of life. That as Jesus became incarnate and dwelt among us, so the whole of reality may be used by God to show forth his love and convey his grace. He can take the ordinary and make it special—he can touch secular things of life and make them sacred. It was true that his love was powerfully expressed in the preaching and people regularly found God in this way. God blessed our weekly Holy Communion together. This act of meeting around his table became more and more special to us. But he used non-religious ways too. Christians simply caring for their neighbours; visiting the bereaved; in fact, simple warm loving Christianity. Through the ordinary contacts of life the gospel was spreading.

As a result, our attitude to spiritual gifts began to change as well. It is all too easy to put certain gifts on a pedestal and think that the really 'souped-up' Christian is one with all kinds of pious blessings.

One way in which we were helped to see that we should not assign gifts to the spiritual realm only was in the area of prophecy. Many churches today have rediscovered the importance of prophecy. For the New Testament, prophecy may be a direct word of challenge, or a word of encouragement and direction, or a word of guidance for the future. As a congregation we had little experience of prophecy, and like most Christians we were wary of 'nut-cases' getting on their own hobby horses. But the leadership had agreed that if we really desired to be open to the Spirit, we should be willing to allow the use of his gifts among us. Indeed, we felt, it should be encouraged and tested.

One day we were taken up on this. Just before a Sunday morning service, a young man, Andy, asked me if I would allow him to give a prophecy. I gulped; 'Does it *have* to be this morning?' 'Yes,' said Andy emphatically, 'I really feel that God has a message for us all.' I was very tempted to ask him what he thought the point of the sermon was, but I wisely dropped this tempting question. 'All right, Andy,' I said drawing a deep breath, 'the best place is after my sermon and before the prayers.' Inwardly I groaned; 'Help! What on earth have I let us all in for!'

But a remarkable thing occurred that morning. We were in the middle of a sermon series based on Michael Harper's helpful book, *Let My People Grow*. As I prepared my sermon in the week, I intended in the conclusion to challenge us all concerning our love and support of one another. Although there was a much deeper fellowship than before, we were still existing as individual Christians and really sacrificial sharing was rare. But for some reason or another, I failed to make the challenge I intended. I didn't do it deliberately, because when I stepped down from the pulpit I was inwardly kicking myself for omitting this challenge. I couldn't understand it—did I side-step a potentially divisive subject subconsciously?

Whatever the cause of that extraordinary omission, God came to the rescue with the prophecy brought by Andy. As he spoke apparently from God, he emphasized the very point I was intending to make. 'You say you love one another and care for one another, but I know that in this congregation there is much loneliness and hurt that is not shared. You carry your needs, guilt and fear away, not realizing that you are a healing community. My children! I call upon you to love one another as brothers and sisters—to share in deeper ways than you have ever done; to be reckless in your love for me and others.' Even the same verses of Scripture I was going to use in my application came out in Andy's prophecy. It was an amazing 'coincidence'. A few folk after the service said how the sermon and the prophecy linked together. That was our first experience of prophecy and it taught a few, especially me, not to be so sceptical.

But there was a more ordinary form of prophecy we stumbled on as well—one that was no less God-given. This experience made me realize that within the Christian family, in the Holy Spirit, we do not have to restrict prophecy to someone standing up in church and using a set introduction: 'Thus says the Lord.'

It happened in this way. Soon after Andy's prophecy we had a Church Council Day Conference. Our subject for the first session was 'Our dream for the future'. I reminded the members that we should be a spiritual, caring fellowship. And then three members of the Council outlined briefly what their hope was for the church. Peter Green, who was one of the three, gave a short but powerful outline of his 'dream' of the future which was truly prophetic. It was to be a word which was to shape all that we planned and prayed for. He said very movingly that 'Jesus is for everybody'. Not just for church people, nor for religious, middle-aged, middle-class people—but for everyone. Were we, in fact, concerned about 'everyone'? Did our concerns reach to the homeless, to the social misfits, to those who work in the Post Office, Boots, Woolworths, Marks and Spencers and other stores? It was an important prophetic challenge, even though we did not call it that, but as a vision it played a cardinal role in shaping our conscious plans for the development of the building later. As such it was a reminder to me particularly that in a God-conscious community, prophecy is very much in evidence and it does not have to have a label to function as prophecy.

If God was opening our eyes to the way he used the ordinary things and happenings of life to speak, he was also showing us that renewal by the Holy Spirit was essentially renewal in the Trinity, as each person of the Godhead plays his role in our lives, so becoming more personal and special to us. I have noted that quite a few people who have been influenced through charismatic renewal have remarked that, 'I think I now have a much deeper appreciation of the Trinity since I experienced renewal in the Spirit!' This, in fact, should be the case. The role of the Holy Spirit according to Scripture is to make the work of Jesus real to us. Some Christians wear the badge of the Dove proudly, but let us be warned—this is not a good symbol of Christianity. The Holy Spirit is distressed when Jesus is obscured and the spotlight falls on him. There is no salvation and certainly no fullness of blessing except through Jesus: it is the Holy Spirit's job and joy to apply the mighty acts of the cross and resurrection to our lives.

This is not, of course, to denigrate the renewal movement—far from it. As the Father's gift of life, the Spirit becomes the bond of love between the Godhead and us and we are drawn into the Father's presence by him, exclaiming, 'Abba! Father!' He builds us up into Christ and gives us the gifts of our inheritance in Christ. So we should find in the normal Christian life the whole action of the Trinity: the Father's love, the Son's work, the Spirit's gifts.

One slightly amusing aspect of this truth, for a number of us who led weekends of renewal and celebration in the North East, was that we usually found ourselves stressing the theme of the lordship of Jesus. It became a standing joke among us whether the next theme was going to be 'Jesus is Lord' or 'The Lord is Jesus' or 'Is Jesus Lord?' or 'Christ the Lord!' At the heart of the quandary was the conviction that the heart of renewal is commitment to Jesus Christ. He is never secondary to any movement of the Spirit. Neither for that matter is the Father. To enter more and more into his love and into the realization of his care is the secret of all spiritually alive people.

As this Trinitarian dimension grew in the congregation, so the gifts of individuals became more prominent in the fellowship—especially that of leadership. In all kinds of ways we noticed God quietly at work. Richard Briggs, our treasurer, felt strongly called to start a Saturday Shop to sell community goods to shoppers. His idea was adventurous to say the least; it was to set up an attractive shop manned by volunteers from the congregation to sell handicrafts made locally by handicapped and disadvantaged people. In time this shop became a bridge between the church and the wider community.

Leardership was being expressed in other ways too. Peter Green shared with me the chairmanship of the Council, and I valued his professionalism and abilities as a leader. But other leaders were beginning to emerge from the congregation. This was mainly due to the Open to God campaign referred to in the previous chapter, and it was most encouraging that people were beginning to take the initiative in many areas of church life. When I arrived in 1975, there were no house groups. Now people were actually offering their services to lead! Ideas for development were no longer coming from just me and a few others. When I started at St Nic's, one of my private moans was, 'What I don't do won't get done!' But it was different now. People like Peter West, David Gregory-Smith and Alison Foote took a marvellous lead in the development of the church as a praying family. My colleague, Pete Broadbent, with John Ledger and a few others were beginning to shake up the organization of the church to make it more efficient. Our preaching team was strengthened by the arrival of a good friend of mine, David Day. David and Rosemary with their three teen-agers had just moved from Nottingham to Durham because David had been appointed to a new post in the Education Department of the University. David's main gift was that of communication. He is one of the most entertaining preachers I know, and it was a great joy to have him with me to share the preaching load.

As all these exhilarating gifts appeared, so I became uncomfortably aware of the challenge this was to me personally. It was all that I wanted—but it threatened me. The concept of 'lay responsibility' was at the heart of my philosophy of the church, but now that it was developing so strongly I felt worried. In a very real way the maturing of Christians was, to some extent, related to my prayers for the congregation ever since my arrival. Very few of the congregation knew that when I locked up the church at the end of the day, I would spend at least fifteen minutes just wandering among the pews one by one. I tried to visualize the congregation sitting in their pews. This wasn't too difficult a thing to do because Church of England folk are creatures of habit—they always sit in the same seats! And I would pray, often aloud, for each member of the family—for those who were unhappy with the change going on, for those with special needs, for those with distinctive gifts. Above all, I prayed for the renewal of the congregation, in the words of Paul, that 'they would grow up in every way to Christ who is the head'.

But now it was happening and every-member ministry was developing, I did not like what was going on in me. It was a delight to see the 'one man band' ministry ending, but it is not always easy for the 'one man' to accept the psychological problem of how to be a member of an orchestra. Some form of death takes place when ministry is shared, I began to find, and I began to understand why some clergy find it so difficult to let go of important aspects of their work, because their self-esteem, dignity and concept of office is bound up with their roles.

It was indeed a delight to have lay folk at last taking over roles that I had done so far, but I began to wonder where I fitted in all this glorious uncertainty. The things I had sole responsibility for, others were now doing, in some cases better than I. In other cases I had entrusted duties to people who were clearly not so capable yet, and it was tempting to wrench it back from them because they were inexperienced. Then it dawned on me what the problem was. I had handed over to others many of the things I was good at. This left me with chores—such as administration—that I was not so good at. My own personal ministry now centred around my weaknesses and not my strengths. Somehow I had to come to terms with this, otherwise my ministry could become soured and restrict the growth of others.

But it is very difficult to share that kind of problem in a parish. How could I say to the team of leaders surrounding me; 'I'm so glad that you have responded with such zeal and ability, but I must now confess that I have a ministerial identity crisis as a result!'

The problem solved itself in St John's College car park! I attended the opening of the new Library, and I met the late Dr Frank Lake, then Director of Clinical Theology. 'How are things going, George?' he asked. 'Fine, Frank,' I replied, 'there has been tremendous encouragement in so many different areas. But I do have a small problem and I would value your comments on it. It's a foolish thing really, and I'm almost embarrassed to ask your opinion, but here goes!

'As the church has grown and leadership has increased, I have handed over to members of my team duties and responsibilities that were formerly mine. Creativity is now team-centred and not just coming from a few of us. I now find myself in the puzzling situation of working from my weaknesses rather than from my strengths. The things I used to reckon I was good at have been taken over by others, leaving me with jobs and chores that I hate doing!'

Frank laughed and said in his characteristic fashion, 'Well, praise God for teaching you the importance of working from weak areas of your ministry! The majority of clergy refuse to allow God to teach them this and they stop growing.'

As Eileen and I drove home I remarked to her, 'Well, Frank wasn't much help. The importance of working from weakness, indeed!' And yet as I began to ponder over it for the first time from a positive point of view, I began to see what Frank meant. It is all too easy to cling to things that we excel in, clasping them to our breast as if for us only, refusing to share or release them. Working from my weakness in ministry might be just the very thing that God wanted for me. If through this I could enable others to grow, then I must be prepared to relinquish even the things that I regarded as the rights of my ministry.

This, I saw, was the ministry of Christ. He did not count

equality with God a thing to be grasped, but emptied himself, taking the form of a 'slave'. Ministry is all about emptying, I realized, and it is better to be a football manager or coach who by sitting on the sidelines is able to release the skills of eleven others, than to be the star player who cracks in all the goals. As I returned from Nottingham I was able to pray silently, 'Thank you, Lord, for allowing me to see the importance of this lesson. Help me to affirm the gifts of others and allow them proper expression in your body. Keep pride, vaingloriing and self-seeking far from me. Help me to delight in the gifts of your Spirit to others.' Although this was not a major personal problem it was a significant factor I had to resolve. It was a bridge crossed: I had to learn that lesson before others could grow.

9

Prison, Praise and People

The church entered 1979 in a buoyant mood. God was gently renewing the structures, raising up leadership and bringing new gifts to his people. As vicar I was thrilled and humbled to see the signs of growth. It was just as well that I had learned the lesson about accepting gladly the leadership of lay folk at all levels of church life, because I was suddenly removed from the fellowship at a most important time.

The phone rang. It was the Chief Prison Officer at Low Newton Remand Centre where I was a part-time chaplain. Low Newton was a small Remand Centre which, as its name indicates, housed young people awaiting trial. On average there were about 320 young men under twenty-one and a small prison for women which could accommodate up to forty. Most of them were habitual offenders, their misdemeanours ranging from petty theft to grievous bodily harm, rape and even manslaughter. 'I'm afraid that the mother of one of our inmates has died. Could you pop in this morning and break the news to her son?' I groaned inwardly, because this was an aspect of the job that I did not like. Although these kids were full of bravado and brag, they did not have the emotional and spiritual resources to take news of sudden death in the family. The lad in question had been in trouble with the police for years and had a long history of violence. But faced with the news, I knew he would crumble like the rest.

It was a bad winter's day when I left home to visit the prison. Snow was drifting across the road and there were warnings of black ice. I was about a mile from the prison, carefully navigating a bend in the road, when I felt the car beginning to slide. Transfixed and helpless, I watched in horror as my small Fiat aimed itself at a Land-rover climbing up the incline towards me. I tried to steer away, but unerringly the Fiat scored a bullseye. There was something comical about the horrified expression on the face of the oncoming driver as I moved in for the kill.

I must have only been out for a few seconds, but I became aware of a voice asking, 'Are you all right? Are you all right?' The concerned face of the Land-rover driver looked down on me through the shattered window. I looked around to see the extent of the damage. Every window was smashed in, and I was lying on my back, still strapped into my seat which was completely broken.

Amazingly, apart from a few cuts to my face and knees, I was more or less unharmed. But my car was a total write-off. So in fact was the Land-rover, although we did not know it at the time. We did the usual things, exchanging names and addresses and details of one another's insurance companies. I was slightly embarrassed to find that I had made the acquaintance of the father of my lad's best friend. Not the best way to pay social calls!

As a result, I never got to the prison that day. After a routine visit to the hospital I was advised to go home and rest for a few days. My troubles began about a week later when I was overcome by the most fearsome headaches accompanied by vomiting which lasted for over twenty-four hours.

This meant that I was not able to chair the crucial Council meeting which was due to meet to discuss the question of the buildings. I had been a member of a small working party which was due to present a proposal to the Church Council, and there I was unable to take part. I could have cancelled the meeting, but my instinct was to let it continue. So it was that the council met in my lounge below to make a decision once and for all concerning our plans for development. Our lay chairman Peter Green took control of the meeting, and this time there was no half-heartedness or hesitation. The Council agreed that God was calling us to renew the buildings. Those present felt sure that the fourteen months away from the scheme had resulted in confirmation that we had to go ahead. The congregation had grown in number, commitment and vision, and it was poised for great things.

After the meeting, Peter popped up to the bedroom and told me the joyful news that the Council wanted to press on with radical plans for development. It was more or less as we had originally planned. 'We had a marvellous meeting,' Peter said, 'we agreed unanimously to accept the working party's proposals. The nave is to be carpeted throughout, chairs will replace the pews, a false ceiling will be put in to conserve heat, the kitchen will be moved to the organ area and an electronic organ console would be free standing in the church.'

Peter continued with his list of improvements to the building. 'We were so sorry not to have you with us for this significant meeting.'

And yet in a way it was strangely appropriate that I was absent from that meeting which gave the go-ahead. It was important for the church not to rely on the clergy. Our discovery of every-member ministry had to result in the role of the lay people making decisions for their own church. It was a great joy to witness the maturation of the fellowship to this extent, even though it was not the most pleasant way for me to spend an evening!

And the church ministered to me in a direct healing

way. Because of the continuing headaches I was admitted to hospital for observation for four days. Upon discharge I was told that the headaches could last with the same intensity for anything up to a year! The Diocese very kindly arranged for me to have a period of convalescence at a nearby retreat house, and before I went away for this break representatives of the congregation laid hands on me for healing during our Communion service. It was a lovely expression of love and concern. I remember thinking at the time; 'I hope it works!'

I went away on my convalescence to the Catholic community and found the experience a deeply helpful time of spiritual refreshment. The Passionist order at Minsteracres was a caring band of priests, nuns and lay brothers whose ministry lay in providing retreat facilities for Christians. Some of them had been influenced by the renewal movement in the Catholic Church, and this showed in their worship as well as their openness to Christians of other denominations. They also prayed that I would recover quickly from the accident. That short stay deepened my appreciation of Catholic Christianity and increased my longing for unity among Christians. How it must break Christ's heart that his people are so scattered and divided! Oh, for men and women of love and faith to thread together the 'seamless' robe of Christ that rigidity, arrogance and intolerance tear apart. 'The nearer we come to Christ, the nearer we come together,' once said the theologian Moltmann. It is about time we discovered that unity in him.

The joyful thing was that over the period of ten days that I spent convalescing, my headaches disappeared, never to return. I returned to work invigorated and whole. The healing that the church had claimed for me was in fact mine, and I was back to normal.

Now that the Council had given the go-ahead for major improvements to the building, we had to mobilize the resources of our lay people to grapple with the task. The architect calmly informed us that the financial target was £150,000. We gulped on hearing this news. We had never had to reach beyond £2,000 for anything! Did we in fact have the commitment to go ahead and the faith to believe that our God answers that kind of prayer?

The architect presented his plans to the congregation at a Parish Half-Day Conference, and receiving the congregation's response the Church Council passed a formal motion endorsing those plans and calling for the appropriate steps to be taken for their immediate implementation. We were off!

Because we felt that it was necessary to harness the gifts of the congregation, six working parties were set up to set things in motion. Fund raising, finance, publicity, furnishings, ministry and a practical group were the six working parties, and members of the congregation were invited to join.

One senior member of the church refused point blank to join the fund-raising team. 'George,' he said, 'I have had long connections with this church over many years, and I have done practically every job there is to do here. So I will tell you confidently that this is a big mistake. You cannot raise £150,000 from this congregation. I am sorry that I cannot help you.' I respected that man's honesty and sincerity. Humanly speaking he had history and economics on his side—but that didn't stop him being completely wrong.

By now we were beginning to learn the secret of prayer. Half-nights of prayer were born and some met early on Thursday and Saturday mornings. We prayed, not to manipulate God, or to convince ourselves that we were doing the right thing, but to lean upon God's resources and to discover his will. Some of the fellowship learned the value of fasting as we dug well-pits of prayer. Not all members of the church were able to attend our extended times of prayer, but that didn't matter. Prayer was beginning to be our central concern and it entered into every aspect of our life. It was not haphazard either. We set prayer goals. We had £150,000 to aim for, for a start. 'Lord,' we prayed, 'we don't know how we can raise this money, but we know that you are God and can provide.'

One member of the church later described these times of prayer as 'adventures in praying'. 'I felt a little like Abraham,' he remarked. 'We were leaving the old securities behind and embarking upon a journey of faith which seemed to go into the unknown. All we had to go on was our instinct that God was calling us to go out. We began to learn the most elementary lessons of Sunday-school Christianity—that God could be trusted!'

But our energies were not tied down completely to the Building Project. By now our dance and drama groups were quite experienced and professional. Our drama duo, New Wine, were also beginning to make their mark, and we were getting many requests to assist churches in the North of England. Our greatest joy was not in helping the affluent and middle-class congregation, but the struggling churches in the mining villages around. Time and again we came across Christians longing for change and asking, 'Why can't it happen here? What do we need to *do* to realize our potential?' Disillusioned clergy would shrug their shoulders and say, 'We tried it all, and it doesn't work!' One vicar told me bleakly, 'I'm here to officiate at a funeral—that of my church. I have not had a new member for eight years. In five years' time they will close us down.'

There is not one simple answer to the cry: 'What can we do?' Each situation is unique and requires its own different approach. Nevertheless I discovered a common malaise in churches that were in advance stages of ecclesiastical terminal illness—lack of vision. Unless the minister and at least some of the people have a spiritual vision which sees beyond the difficulties of the human situation, everything will seem hopeless. Vision thus becomes the driving force of prayer and the wheels of change are set in motion. It is important also for this vision to be shared with others so that it may gently permeate the life of the church, creating expectancy and awareness of what is possible.

I have sometimes been asked how 'vision' is captured. To a great degree genuine spiritual vision is God-given, but it is possible to isolate some of the human elements in it.

First, vision is the opposite of complacency. If Christians are satisfied with things as they are, God's vision of what is possible will not be shared. There has to be a divine discontent with what we find. There must be a desire to share Christ with a broken and fallen world, and there must be a concern for God's honour and glory.

From this will flow, secondly, an openness to new possibilities—even a readiness to consider that God may have to tear down and remove the established and precious symbols of our faith and security. This will, no doubt, mean entering into pain of change—because only rarely will a congregation be united initially in the goal of the vision. A leader with the eye of faith must be prepared to stand alone at times.

Thirdly, if they are God-given such goals we have must be tested by other Christians and shared by them. Whether this group is in the minority or majority makes little substantial difference, as long as the leadership is gripped by it.

Fourthly, deep, committed and urgent prayer will be found to be the living stream which will transform the desert—and make the vision a reality.

On one of our weekends away, we went to minister to a number of churches in Cumbria. A group of Christians from a village asked to see me, and they poured out their complaints about their unsympathetic vicar who did not

want change. 'What can we do?' they asked. I replied
that, to be honest, I just did not know. The situation was
far too complex for a stranger to pontificate about an issue
he knew nothing about. 'But let me suggest a number of
obvious things. First, meet regularly for prayer. And
don't just pray that the vicar will see your point of view—
pray that all of you, together, will discover God's point of
view. Then tell the vicar that you are going to meet
regularly to pray for the work of the church and his work
too. Ask him to join you whenever he can. Also,
encourage him in his ministry. Ask him to share the
difficulties and joys of his work, so that you can pray for
him more intelligently. You never know, you might make
some progress if you try these things.'

A year later, one of the group wrote to me to say that
the advice was followed and it had resulted in some
encouraging growth in the congregation. At first the Vicar
had been suspicious of the group appearing to be a 'holy
huddle', but when he saw their desire to support, he
began to share something of his needs. Through this
partnership of vicar and lay folk, goals were set up which
resulted in increased membership and giving. Prayer and
encouragement were the key there.

Prayer also brought its result in our work in the prison.
Since Pete Broadbent and I took over the chaplaincy of
Low Newton, we depended upon the fellowship for prayer
support. But it was always hard work in the prison and
direct results were few and far between. We took the
services every Sunday and visited every week. And yet it
was very enjoyable work because the folk there were in
very great spiritual need. One could clearly see the truth
of Paul's statement that 'the wages of sin is death'. In this
case death was the inability to combat evil and the lack
of interest in spiritual things. Many a lad confessed to me,
'I wish I could be a different person. I hate myself for
doing these things.'

One afternoon in the summer of 1979, I was driving to the prison and thoroughly depressed by the thought of spending another unrewarding afternoon with people whose horizons were so narrow. 'Lord,' I remember praying silently, 'let's have some action this afternoon. Please let us see signs of your Spirit working there.'

When I entered the gates to collect my keys, Phil who was the officer on duty exclaimed: 'You are popular today. Five people want to see you.' Attached to my keys were five white application forms. 'What are they doing on my key ring? They are normally given to the officer at the Centre.' 'I dunno,' he shrugged, 'maybe they were very keen to see you. You'd better get cracking.'

The first person I called on was Phil. Phil was awaiting trial for causing grievous bodily harm to his own eleven-month-old son. I had met Phil some weeks ago, and we had chatted about his background and problems. He lived with his common-law wife, and one evening she went to a party with some other girls, leaving him to look after their child. The child was suffering with colic at the time and screamed so much, that Phil hurled the child across the room in his desperation and impotence, causing irreparable brain damage. This is one of those crimes which other prisoners find unforgivable. They have their own morality which will allow no forgiveness to child molesters, rapists and homosexuals. For his own protection Phil was therefore separated from the other prisoners under Section 43. The last time I had seen Phil was shortly before my holiday and I had left with him Nicky Cruz's book *Run, Baby, Run*.

'Hello, Phil,' I greeted him as I slammed the heavy cell door behind me. 'What can I do for you?'

'Guess what. I think I am a Christian!' he exclaimed.

'Really?' I said sceptically, 'why do you think that?'

'Well, do you remember the book you lent me? I was really moved by what Nicky Cruz said about Jesus, and I

said the prayer in the book. And as I offered my life to him
to do something with, I felt sure that he came into my life.'

Phil went on to show me the picture of Jesus he had
drawn and two simple poems which expressed his new
faith. 'Have you told anyone about this yet?' 'Only Chris
my wife,' he said. 'Look, here is her letter back to me.'

'Well, Phil,' I said, 'there is no doubt about it. You are
clearly a Christian. Welcome to the family!' And in that
cell we prayed together that Phil would grow into the new
life which Christ promises to those who follow him, and
that he would know the freedom that barbed wire and
barred windows couldn't restrict. Indeed, in a later note
to me, Phil wrote: 'Now that Jesus Christ is my friend I am
more free than I have ever been in my life.'

I was on cloud nine when I left Phil's pad and went to
chat to the second lad on my list. Bill was doing six months
for car stealing. He too was in his cell reading a book I had
given him a few weeks before. I recognized the cover: it
was David Wilkerson's famous book, *The Cross and the
Switchblade.*

'Good book, eh, Bill?'

'Great!' he said, 'Do you know, I was really struck by
what you and your curate have been saying about Jesus
Christ. I read this book, and it explained how I can
become a Christian. I said a prayer about letting Jesus
into my heart. But could you explain more?'

Bill and I talked for the next half hour or so about the
Christian faith and we prayed together. As I normally do,
I asked Bill to pray to God in his own words. And in very
simple words Bill thanked God for making him a Christian.

By now I was on cloud ten! This was too good to be
true! I couldn't believe it was happening. Number three
on my list was a young man I did not know. Les had been
sentenced to further Borstal training and he was over at the
workshop. I called him out and we walked around the
grounds and chatted about the Christian faith. 'I don't

know how to begin,' he said awkwardly, 'but on Sunday, a group of young people came to take the service in the morning. Afterwards I borrowed a book from them called *Run, Baby, Run*. The service impressed me very much. We gave those kids a hard time, laughing at them, but I knew they had something we didn't have. Will you tell me something more about the Christian faith?' Les and I went to my office and we talked and prayed over this together.

By now I half expected what my number four client was going to say. To say that I was excited was the understatement of the year. It was a miracle—completely unexpected and almost uncanny. Indeed, the wildest thoughts entered my head about this strange afternoon. Could it be a deliberate plot to 'send up' the Chaplain? No, that was out of the question. These were lads who did not know one another.

Number four was Paul. Paul was a half-caste who unlike the others had at least a Christian background, although he had rejected his faith years ago. I had met him a few times. He had a long history of violence and was also on a GBH charge. Like Les, Paul had been deeply challenged by the group of young Christians from the Methodist Church who had visited the establishment on the previous Sunday. He too borrowed a Christian book, this one by an ex-prisoner called Fred Lemon, and he had taken the step of faith into the kingdom of heaven. Just to confirm that this was real and not just a passing phase I asked him to tell me in his own words what prompted this change of attitude. 'I guess it is the fact that places like this are so soulless. There is no love here—only greed, selfishness and brutality. Those kids seemed to love us. And that book by Fred Lemon pointed me to search for God. I don't think I found him—he found me!'

Number five was Joe. Joe had been a member of a small Bible study group we had begun a few months before and as a result of that service, which had so moved the other two lads, he too had borrowed a Christian book. Joe was still in the enquiring stage and we chatted together for a long time about the meaning of life and the importance of Jesus Christ. He could not accept the resurrection, and this became the centre of our discussion. But a few days later, he too was to find the reality of Jesus Christ.

I returned home four hours later dazed and humbled. Never had I experienced such a time of seeing God at work in that place. There was neither rhyme nor reason to it. The human links were so feeble and tenuous, but God took them and used them greatly. It showed above all the way that Christian literature can be used when it expresses the attractiveness of Jesus Christ. It was a lesson to me never to underestimate the power of God to bring something out of nothing. Although, as it turned out, nothing like that ever happened again in my experience, we did begin to see a trickle of people finding the reality of God in that place. And at the heart of it all was the effectiveness of prayer as the church upheld our ministry in that prison. They too rejoiced greatly when they heard of the events that Thursday afternoon. But sadly, I was not able to keep in touch with the five for very long. I had only a few weeks with them to help them to grow in the Christian life before they were sent off to other institutions. Their names were given to other Chaplains to follow up, but I am trusting that their names are written in the Book of Life.

IO

Miracle at Easter

As commitment to the building project grew in the congregation, so inevitably news of what we were about to
embark upon leaked out to the press. The leading
Northern paper, *The Northern Echo*, heralded it as 'the
most ambitious scheme yet attempted by a parish church
in the North of England'.

There was no doubt about it: hardened agnostic
journalists and reporters found the project quite beyond
their understanding. They were impressed that, at last,
the church was attempting to do something that was useful
and relevant, but the size of the undertaking left them
gasping. 'How much money have you in the kitty?' asked
a young lady reporter well-known as a Marxist.

'About £3,000 at the moment,' I answered.

'And you expect to raise £150,000 from your congregation?' she asked disbelievingly.

Gerald Blake, who was acting as our press officer,
replied, 'Well, it does take some believing, we admit. But
without wishing to sound too pious, we believe that God
has called us to do this project and he has already answered
many of our prayers. Yes, we'll raise it!'

But we knew that it would not get done by doing
nothing. One of my favourite Christmas cracker mottoes

is: 'He who is resting upon his laurels—is wearing them in the wrong place!' I have long been convinced that the modern church has been bedevilled not so much by lack of faith as by lack of energy. Inertia is the modern Christian's besetting sin. 'Faith without works is dead' is good New Testament theology, and we knew that we could not expect God to answer prayer unless we were prepared to go flat out.

Part of our job, therefore, was to find ways of raising money. Realistically we knew that £150,000 was beyond the resources of the congregation even though the vast majority of it had to come from us. It was imperative, therefore, that at some stage we should go to the general public to get support. Our problem was that we could not have chosen a worse time to launch an appeal; inflation was very high and unemployment was on the increase.

Some of our ideas for raising cash were magnificent and showed the creative energies of the congregation. Clive, one of our younger leaders, offered to run a Christmas Fayre which eventually brought in £1,100. Although the amount was a drop in the ocean, its significance lay in drawing together the talents of the congregation in a common cause. There are Christians who dismiss this kind of money raising as somehow unspiritual. I'm afraid I cannot agree with that point of view. It is only unspiritual if people rely on such activities as the sole way of raising money. The main value of such enterprises lies in harnessing the resources of people who would not otherwise be able to contribute through direct giving. I found that old-age pensioners and others were grateful for this kind of activity because at least they could donate some groceries, home-made produce or give a little of their time in manning a stall.

My contribution to the Fayre took the form of running a stall I called the 'Serendipity Stall'. The word 'serendipity' means 'making a happy discovery by accident' and we hoped that this would be true of my stall.

One man who bought something from me asked, 'Do you really think that you are going to raise £150,000 then?'

'I know for a fact we can't,' I replied, 'but we believe that God can provide.'

'Well,' he said, 'you are a vicar, aren't you, and you are supposed to say things like that.'

'I tell you what,' I said jocularly, 'you come to the church in, say, eighteen months' time and see for yourself whether I am right or you are. It might change your mind about God.'

Our fund-raising ideas took many forms and were spread out over the following two years. Evelyn Gibson, our enterprising old-age pensioners, had a brilliant idea which caught the imagination of Durham and brought in well over £1,000. She arranged for the local Territorial Army branch to erect an assault course in the parish and she visited firms and shops in the district to enter teams and to sponsor them. Only Evelyn had the nerve and the charm to cast her spell over the Army and firms alike, and everyone had a great afternoon out, getting muddy and wet.

Another energetic idea came from Tony, one of our Watersports team. He suggested a ten-mile fun run. To our amazement this really caught on, and it was great to see people of all ages run, jog, walk and even crawl around the course. Even I had a go, but it had to be admitted that there was a congregation of very sleepy people that evening.

But the fund-raising scheme which attracted the widest publicity and which was the most ingenious, came from Kevin who got wind of news that the prestigious United States Air Force Band in Europe was visiting the United Kingdom. He wrote to the organizer and got this splendid band to give us a free concert in Durham Cathedral. The

Cathedral was packed for that occasion, and the band gave us a brilliant concert which featured many of the Glen Miller tunes with which the band was identified.

Such events as these were great occasions of fellowship and added to the appeal of our project, but the hard fact we had to face was that the amount of money raised by such special events was infinitesimal compared with our target. Their value lay in creating interest in the project, and in bringing the congregation together. But such events as these got fewer and fewer because the energy invested in them was out of proportion to the cash result. Nevertheless, we had enormous fun in doing things together and it was an example of a happy Christian family serving Christ and enjoying one another's company. Who says that the Christian faith is a dull and miserable affair? We were learning that having fun and laughing together was not incompatible with following Christ. It even brought outsiders to him as well, who were attracted by joyful Christians. I, for one, was delighted to be associated with this 'happy band of pilgrims'.

But while the church was girding up its loins to raise money, storm clouds were gathering over one issue, namely the organ. Although the majority of the congregation liked the plans for change and wanted a modern, bright and comfortable building which could be used seven days a week, there were considerable hesitations about the organ. The problem was that our present instrument was a very fine organ virtually installed singlehanded by Tom, our organist. It was, however, coming up for a major re-fit, and a lot of money would have to be spent on it. Everyone agreed reluctantly that it had to be disposed of and a new organ purchased. And that is where the controversy began.

Tom and many others wanted a pipe-organ to be installed in the new building. But to our horror we discovered that an equivalent pipe-organ would cost over

£90,000! Those of us who bore the responsibility of leadership were convinced that it was totally wrong to spend such a large proportion of our money on an organ. It was the ministry of the church that counted and the organ had to take its place as an element within the total plan, not the deciding factor around which other elements would have to fit. For this reason we felt that we did not have any choice but to go for a good electronic organ.

In order to bring everyone as fully as possible into the discussion of this emotive issue we arranged for outings to churches which had good electronic organs. But feeling was so high on this matter that we knew that the forthcoming Annual General Meeting of the church would be a lively affair with a large number arguing the case for a pipe-organ.

'An electronic organ?' scoffed one person, 'I can just see Tom sitting on his console emerging from the floor of the church like one of the old cinema organs.' Good humoured laughter greeted this contribution, but it was echoed by another person: 'But an electronic organ sounds dreadful. We must have a good organ. It mustn't sound like a Yamaha with boogie woogie sounds.'

The level of discussions soon improved and we were able to see that a significant minority were hesitant about an electronic organ for a variety of reasons. For some there was an honourable reason, that we needed to go for a musical excellence which, in their opinion, meant getting a good organ. But for others, a pipe-organ represented the last bastion of unchanging worship, a symbol of stability and accepted Anglican norms. The discussion over the organ represented our last battle about priorities. It was important that no one single church element should predominate. Even good things can become idols when exaggerated out of proportion.

Mrs Craggs, our assistant organist, whose family had long associations with St Nic's, was forthright in her opinion. She, more than anyone present, showed us the way through the difficulties that evening. She stood there, a vigorous godly lady in her seventies, and in her broad Geordie accent said, 'I love our present organ. And Tom has done a splendid job over these years keeping it going. I like pipe-organs too. You can't beat them. But the organ, like an organist, is a servant of the church. We have to face facts; we cannot spend so much money on a pipe-organ. If we vote tonight for an electronic organ, I for one will go along with the majority vote and support the decision wholeheartedly.'

The vote was taken and by a substantial majority the congregation decided to have an electronic organ in the new building. That was an important decision and it was settled amicably even though feelings had run high during the meeting. But the real importance lay in our refusal to allow the issue of the organ to divert us from our priorities in ministry. We were learning Cowper's spiritual principle:

> Every idol I have known,
> Whate'er that idol be,
> Help me to tear it from thy throne
> And worship only thee.

But we were not finished with the organ. In the Church of England, permanent changes to the fabrics of a church require the permission of the Diocesan Advisory Committee (DAC). And major changes, such as ours, have to receive the permission also of the Chancellor of the Church of England. To our consternation we learned that the Chancellor had refused to allow us to have an electronic organ, and had decreed that we must continue to use a pipe-organ.

We were convinced that this was a mistake and we asked to see the DAC, fairly sure that the Chancellor's verdict had been influenced by them. John Ledger, our newly appointed Chairman of the building project, explained why we had chosen an electronic organ in our plans. 'We appreciate the concerns that many have expressed about an electronic organ. But please, don't allow your attention to concentrate on the organ. Our concern is about the church's witness to the world around. In terms of the things we want to provide, we just do not feel that spending nearly £100,000 on a pipe-organ is good use of money.'

'But Durham is an important ecclesiastical centre,' said a senior clergyman, 'We just cannot allow electronic organs to be installed in a city-centre church. We have to think of future-generations of worshippers.'

David Gregory Smith, our other leader present, then very firmly, but politely, responded, 'I wonder if you have really considered the full implications of our scheme. If it were our intention for our church to be an important ecclesiastical centre, with a fine choir with a reputation for choral singing, then we would certainly want to install a fine pipe-organ. But there are churches already providing that kind of ministry in Durham. We cannot and do not want to compete with the cathedral. Our task is to be a city-centre church which caters for people and seeks to provide a centre for a serving, caring Christianity. We don't want to spend an enormous sum of money on an organ because it will stop us providing other facilities which we feel are more important.'

To our relief, the DAC reluctantly agreed and we were allowed to include an electronic organ in our plans. It is one of those ironies that the organ we eventually got for a little over £15,000 turned out to be so good that many local organists came to regard it as the second best organ in Durham—second only to the one in the Cathedral! Our biggest sorrow was the limited vision of the DAC who, though it consisted of intelligent and godly church people, were so concerned about the organ that they failed to appreciate the vision and enterprise of a congregation who were embarking upon a most radical experiment in ministry.

My two lay colleagues were shattered that not one of the clergy present at that meeting, which included a retired bishop, had appeared to grasp the vision which compelled us to go forward. Whereas many non-church goers were enthusiastically in favour of the project, here was a group of leading church people who did not have one word of encouragement for us. It was sad to discover that this important Advisory Committee was so concerned to maintain an accepted ecclesiastical 'status quo' that it did not appear to be able to enter into the vision of a church that was at least trying to grapple with the first task of the Christian faith, to share its life with others.

But at least we were now able to turn our attention to the task of raising the enormous sum of money. One burning question which none of us could answer at the moment was—to what extent was the congregation behind the project? We knew that the majority had indicated their support, but when translated into cash, how committed were they? The Council had decided to launch our Planned Giving Campaign on Ash Wednesday and our first Gift Day was to be on Easter Sunday. John Ledger in sharing this with the congregation one Sunday morning said, 'No appeal will be made outside our fellowship until after our own Gift Day. We must begin with ourselves. We cannot expect others to give generously until we are prepared to back it wholeheartedly.'

So during the first part of 1980, we tried to ensure that everyone understood the vision behind the building project. Somehow we had to get people to realize fully that the building itself was not the important thing. It was God's mission which counted, and this involved us in a two-fold renewal of people and possessions. A prophecy given in one of our morning services reminded us that

God promises to provide all that his people need to be living stones in his church. If we relied on his resources the project would create a living community as well as a new building.

As Easter Day approached, excitement and anxiety mounted. As vicar I was only too aware of the weakness of the congregation. I was in a better situation than anyone else to know the hesitations of some, the poverty of many, the hardness, apathy, and resistance of a few, as well as the commitment of others. The consequences of failure would be horrific. We had started something which could not easily stop now. But at the very least, our first Gift Day on Easter Sunday would show whether the congregation was really behind the project, or whether it was merely a dream of a few idealists whose imaginations were bigger than their brains.

At breakfast on Easter morning Eileen asked, 'What's your guess? What amount do you think will come in today?'

'I really will be cock-a-hoop if the congregation give £30,000,' I said, 'but I fear it could be well short of that. What do you think?'

'Mm—my guess is about £35,000,' speculated Eileen. 'Like you I can't see our present congregation giving much beyond that.'

We had a lovely Communion service that morning. I preached on the reality of Christ living in a congregation and there was a real spirit of joy and expectancy among us.

'After the service, coffee will be served in the hall while the collection is being counted,' I announced. 'If you want to wait to see how much has been given to the project, please stay behind.'

Most of the congregation waited after the service while the gifts were being counted. We had invited giving for the project in three main ways; through direct giving, through covenants or, for those who could not do either of these, pledges which they promised to pay within a year or two.

It is very hard to say how many had given towards the Project. There was at that time a committed nucleus of about forty people, a lot of interested people, bemused people, penniless but prayerful people, a small nucleus of students....

Voices were hushed when Geoff Moore our church warden came in with the result. 'Everyone will be pleased to know that the giving this morning is £99,942. This is absolutely amazing. Thanks be to God!'

Gasps of amazement echoed around the church, and quite spontaneously we burst into the doxology, 'Praise God from whom all blessings flow!' There were not many dry eyes in church at that moment. We are not the most emotional of congregations, but most of us were profoundly moved by this staggering response. Within a few minutes someone wrote a cheque for £58, and our first Gift Day stood at £100,000. What a response from a fairly ordinary congregation. Praise God indeed!

Gerald Brooke, a former church warden, later commented to me: 'I can recall many an occasion counting £7 or £8 in the collection. To count £100,000 is a miracle beyond my experience and knowledge.' And so it was for us all. By the end of the day our gifts had risen to £101,500. And we all went home to our beds with a great sense of exhilaration and joy. It had been a memorable Easter Day which we will never forget. Surely the risen Christ stood among us that day! Indeed, we felt a little like the first disciples who said to Thomas, who had missed all the excitement of the first resurrection day, 'You missed something last Sunday. We met Jesus—he is raised from the dead.' So we said to members of our fellowship who were away that weekend, 'If only you had been with us on Easter Day. The sense of awe, the wonder and jubilation when we realized that the giving was £100,000!'

In actual fact the true significance of the money lay in the fact that it told us something very important about the congregation! Up to that point we had no yardstick to go by. We had no way of telling if the project committee was out on a limb. Our first Gift Day was a major turning point—it declared convincingly that the commitment which had not been in the congregation a few years before was clearly here now. We now knew for sure that God wanted us to go ahead.

Indeed, for some of us the day represented a kind of psychological beginning of the end. We only had £50,000 to go. We were almost home and dry!

II

Pull Us Out—It's Madness!

The months that followed that magnificent Easter Day were filled with optimism and purpose. The first Gift Day seemed to be such a massive vote of confidence in the project that a successful outcome appeared to be inevitable. We restarted the Friday lunches in May, and every day something seemed to be happening in the church. It was true that the architect had written to say that the newly estimated costs could be as high as £200,000, but this did not stem the quiet feeling of elation that was running throughout the congregation. A number of us were slightly worried by the suggestion that the project might be as high as that. I was personally determined to keep it as near to £150,000 as possible because this was the figure we had originally told the congregation, and I did not want to break faith with them.

At the beginning of July, the project committee met with Ronald Sims (our architect) and his quantity surveyor, to receive tenders for the project. We had been looking forward to this meeting for some time, eager to have exact costings for the work to proceed.

As soon as we were seated, Ronald cleared his throat and looked uncomfortably around. 'I am very sorry to have to tell you that I have very bad news for you. You are not going to like what I have to say. The fact of the matter is that because of soaring costs the lowest estimate is £373,000 and the highest is £463,000. This came as a major shock to me, I had no idea.'

We were devastated.

'But how is it possible for the cost to be as high as that?' interrupted a member. 'We were told the scheme would cost about £150,000, and now we are told it is going to cost more than twice as much!'

'Of course, a true picture does not emerge until this point,' Ronald explained. 'My figures were based upon past experience. It is clear that costs have risen faster than anyone dreamed possible.'

'Well, it is equally plain that we cannot entertain such colossal expenditure,' added someone. 'It would be beyond reasonable expectations to assume that the congregation can reach even the lowest estimate.'

It was with a feeling of despondency and discouragement that the committee agreed that none of the tenders were acceptable. Instead a small group of us was asked to consider ways of reducing the high costs while trying to retain the essential character of our scheme.

'Let's call the whole church together to pray this over,' suggested Alison Moore. 'Yes,' agreed another, 'we must get all our groups together and share the problem with them.'

Many phone calls were made over the next few days, and about seventy of us met in the church on Thursday evening following that meeting, to pray about the problems. John Ledger explained the nature of the problem, and I spoke for a little while about the way that God provides. I drew a parallel with the early Christian church. 'The faith of the early Christians after Pentecost,' I said, 'met with many retreat points and discouragements. I am sure that many must have felt like giving up. At times like that they had to reach beyond their own resources to

God's. We are in that position now. We need to discover his will and have the courage to follow it.'

We prayed together and sang for quite a while as well. Never had our praying been as urgent and as perplexed as that evening. And as our praying continued, a remarkable transition occurred during that time. Gradually, without any artificial division of the time, our prayers changed from petition to praise. People began to thank God for his goodness to us in Christ and his goodness to us as a church. They actually began to thank him for this new challenge that would enable us to see the power of God. Our attention consequently shifted from our need to his greatness and sovereignty. And we ended our meeting by singing one of our favourite songs, 'Jehovah Jireh, my provider, his grace is sufficient for thee, for thee.' We left that prayer evening quite sure that we had to persevere with the project, but equally sure that we had to find ways of reducing the enormous tenders.

Over that summer, a number of the team worked almost night and day on the plans, seeking ways of saving money without destroying our concept of having a modern building that would serve the community. We decided that the Church Council should be called for an extraordinary meeting towards the end of August to consider the options open to us.

'A number of us have met frequently over the summer,' explained Geoff Moore to the assembled Council, 'and we have reduced the lowest estimate quite considerably, but it still gives us the essential project.'

'But what exactly have you been able to cut out?' asked someone.

'Well, we thought there were many savings we could make by doing things ourselves. For example, we could do the entire decoration of the halls. We could strip the church and make it ready for the builders. But there are other things that would bring a considerable saving—such as the false ceiling. That really is a luxury.'

'And what would be the cost of this reduced scheme?' asked a member.

Geoff looked uncomfortable at this question because he knew that the answer would horrify some. 'We estimate that it is in the region of £260,000.'

'£260,000!' gasped someone, 'it is still much higher than we expected. We know that God is calling us to do something. But I really do question if this is it.'

It was in some ways quite extraordinary how we could plummet from the heights of Easter Day to our present anxiety and fear. Nevertheless, it was agreed after lengthy discussion that we should make sure that the church family knew all the details of our predicament. A further Gift Day was planned for the end of September, and we decided that another Council meeting should be called for October 1st, at which we would make a final decision whether or not to proceed with the main contract. In the meantime, we also decided that as the church roof had to be done urgently, we would move out of the church into the nearby Town Hall for a temporary period, while the roof was reslated.

At the Council's request, I wrote a letter of encouragement and challenge to each member of the congregation. 'We have reached a point of realism with the project,' I wrote. 'It now looks certain that the scheme is going to cost very much more than we expected. It would be very tempting to pull back now and only do minor improvements. But many of us are convinced that God is still calling us to press on and bring this project about. Let's not be discouraged but reach out in faith to the inexhaustible riches in Christ.'

In response to this, one Church Council member who had long expressed anxieties about the scheme wrote his own open letter to the congregation saying that he was convinced we ought not to go ahead, but should turn our energies away from the building to a greater care for people. Of course, that was what the scheme was about! Our present facilities made caring for people well nigh impossible. We were all sad when the same member resigned from the Council because he could not conscientiously go along with our decisions, although he still remained an active and loyal member of the congregation. But it showed the deep levels of anxiety that were running through the fellowship.

Up to this point I was fairly unperturbed by the turmoil. I knew of the anxieties and sympathized with those who did not want the project to get out of control. But suddenly I found myself under considerable pressure from frantic people who wanted me to stop what they thought to be a disastrous course of action.

One couple who came to see me were quite adamant concerning the plight they saw ahead. The husband was an astute businessman who also knew the congregation well. He had worked out that there were less than forty people in the congregation with decent salaries. The rest consisted of old-age pensioners, students, and people mortgaged up to their eye-balls. 'George,' he said, 'I have been fully behind the project from the beginning—you know that. But I am seriously worried by the enormous increase in the cost of the scheme. When it was £150,000, I knew we could reach that with a gigantic struggle. But we cannot reach double that figure. Look, here are my deductions produced on the basis of the membership of the church as it is now. I don't need to argue with you, the facts are there. We are pleading with you as our vicar— pull us away from the brink before it is too late. Only you can do it—it's madness to go forward.'

Within the same week, another businessman came to see me. He was a middle-aged man who had only recently joined our fellowship and he was visibly growing as a Christian. Although he was exhilarated to be part of a fellowship struggling to show the relevance of the Christian faith, he too was now very troubled by the prospect of disaster looming ahead. His professional expertise lay in dealing with liquidated companies and he could see so many parallels between our situation and the struggling companies he was trying to rescue from liquidation.

'I don't want to sound like a Jeremiah,' he began, 'but let me explain what will happen to us if we are not careful. From the moment that the builders start we shall have to make monthly payments to them. We shall then have exhausted our cash assets within six months and after that we shall be in the hands of banks, incurring an ever increasing debt from interest charges which we shall not be able to pay off. Now, if that doesn't scare you, it certainly scares me to death!'

I was being scared to death more by the number of people coming to me with warnings similar to the fears of the two men mentioned. As is often the case I too began to waver and to have serious misgivings about the amount we were considering. Was it right to go ahead when the costs were so staggeringly high? Were we in danger of emulating the disastrous charge of the Gadarene swine, 'any way as long as it is forward'?

In the New Testament, mention is made of the gift of faith as one of the gifts of the Spirit. This gift is clearly not the same as that of saving faith, without which no one becomes a Christian. The gift of faith in Paul's teaching appears to be the power to believe in God's promises. To my rescue, and indeed to the rescue of a number of us at that time, came a member of the leadership who I think was given that gift for this very special moment. Peter West was at that time our other church warden, with Geoff Moore. Peter had always been one of our prayer leaders. By nature he is a quiet, reflective, pastoral man who prefers to take an unobtrusive role in the leadership of the team. At this juncture, he showed the most tremendous confidence in God, just as a number of us were wavering and having second thoughts. Peter would be the first to express surprise that it was a special gift of faith that was given to him—but I have no doubt. He was given and showed amazing assurance that we were doing the right thing. Because I was being battered by people who had no one but me to turn to, quite naturally I too was beginning to question the wisdom of the project. I came perilously close to pulling the plug on the whole thing, and I would have done had it not been for Peter, who at this point took such a commanding role in this area of believing prayer.

But I was not the only one in the leadership team having a bad patch at this crucial time. As I was at the heart of the pastoral relationships I was struck by the fact that nearly half of the project committee were suffering from personal crises of one sort or another. One was caught up in a relationship with a woman which threatened to ruin his marriage and involvement in church life; another was having serious problems at home; another was worried about his future; another was under stress in his work situation; another was suffering from recurrent illness in his family. It appeared very remarkable that it happened all together. I am not the kind of person to go looking for demons under beds, neither do I believe that everything has to have a spiritual or demonic origin. It could well be a coincidence, but we had to entertain the possibility that, if God was attempting to build his kingdom among us, someone deeply involved in the eternal struggle between good and evil did not like what was going on. At the very least, we had to be on our guard and defend one another in prayer.

The leader who was ensnared in an embarrassing liaison with another woman came to share the problem with me. He was a happily married man who had a responsible and demanding job. His work had brought him into close contact with a female colleague who was trying to entice him into a relationship which would have ruined him. He knew all too well the consequences if he succumbed. The pressure from this woman was considerable and he came very close to leaving his wife. But he was spiritually mature enough to recognize what was happening to him and his marriage, and after talking it through with his wife, who could probably see more clearly than he the tightrope he was walking, he came to share it with me. We were able to pray it through and talk about it. Both of us were able to see that the problem was far greater than mere infatuation. The pressure of his work situation together with the demands of the building project indicated that the problem was a spiritual one. It was a real joy to see this man acquiring the moral strength to turn his back on that woman who was threatening to destroy all that he stood for. He said to me later, 'If there had not been spiritual growth and renewal in the congregation, I would not have found the support, love and forgiveness to prevent residual bitterness. The amazing thing,' he continued, 'is that I had no peace and assurance until I took the step of breaking with that woman. When I did so, I was able to return to the Lord in repentance and discovered again the strengthening hand of the Lord and an infilling of the Spirit in my life.'

It was a lesson that we had to support one another. Lonely Christians are defenceless Christians, because they are weak in their isolation. We were beginning to discover the power in Christian fellowship. Christ did not make us his body because it seemed a good idea at the time. He made us his body because we need him and one another in order to grow in the Christian life. A song we began to learn at this time spoke to those of us in leadership:

Guard your circles, brother,
Keep your armour bright,

Satan cannot break the bond in which you stand,
Joy is the food we share, love is our home, brothers,
Praise God for the Body. Shalom, shalom.

While the leadership was being rocked by external problems during this time, the congregation was still very unsettled about the project. The earlier euphoria had given way to considerable heartsearching and hesitation. The voices of those who wanted minor improvements were now dominant.

Harvest Sunday arrived, and we had our second Gift Day as we had planned. During the morning service the dance group gave us a challenging and helpful mime. They explained to me before the service that they wanted to make a contribution on the theme of giving and they intended to explore the different ways people give to God—resentfully, boastfully, painfully, noisily, sacrificially, and so on. Because it was Harvest, they decided to use different size marrows to convey the spirit of giving. The music group supplied the background music, and it was an effective and very funny portrayal of giving. The final words of the mime were those of Jesus in Mark 12:41 about the widow, who with her tiny offering, gave all she possessed. In the mime she was the one who offered a small courgette to the Lord! Through this mime the congregation were reminded that it is the sacrificial offering that God accepts.

At the end of Harvest Sunday, another £28,000 was given and £17,000 loaned, bringing the gross fund to £154,000. It was amazing to see this money coming in from substantially the same people, who had given so generously a few months earlier. A stranger who was with us in the evening service was clearly overcome by this giving and was heard to say, 'Where is it coming from? I can't understand it!'

And neither could we. God was so good to us and yet

there were those who were still not convinced that this constituted a divine 'go ahead' for the project. There was still a heart of unbelief among some in the congregation. 'It is a magnificent response,' said someone, 'but it is coming from the same people. We have squeezed them dry. They cannot possibly give any more.' And yet, in making that kind of judgement such people had already overlooked the fact that, a few months before, no one would have believed it possible that a smallish congregation such as ours could have raised £154,000 in less than six months. Christians have to learn the lesson of faith over and over again.

The Church Council meeting took place on October 1st, and while we met, many of the congregation also assembled in small groups to pray. This was going to be the moment of truth that would show the calibre of our faith. Were we going to dangle our toes in the river Jordan, so to speak, and decide that life in Egypt is preferable to crossing—or were we going to advance across our Jordan into the promised land? One of our leaders who was at that Council meeting said to me later that, for him, that was the most important meeting he had ever had. He was shivering from fear, he said, in case the Council decided to turn its back on the project as it had done so a few years before.

We discussed seven options, ranging from doing nothing to accepting the scheme. We discussed and argued for three hours. It was the most honest meeting I have ever attended. Our fellowship and love had deepened to such an extent, and we had grown so clearly in Christian maturity, that we could share frankly and fully together. The fears as well as the faith and hope were publicly admitted. We could all see very clearly the difficulties ahead in raising a sum in the region of £260,000. Nevertheless, we wanted to find and do the will of God.

After three hours of inconclusive discussion, we turned

to a time of unhurried prayer and then the motion was put to press ahead with a building scheme. We do not usually vote in our Council meetings, but as this was a legal matter we decided to record the votes, and the voting showed a massive desire to accept the motion to press on with the project. It was also agreed that we should sign the contract with the building firm so that the work could begin at once. And the Council dispersed to their homes, knowing that the destiny of the church had been shaped that evening for perhaps the next hundred years or so. At last the way was open—this time there could be no turning back.

12

Exile

It was a bright Saturday in September when we started to strip the church. This was one way we had estimated that we could save money, so forty of us went down to move out the furniture, the pews, the sanctuary furnishings—everything, in fact, that could be moved. There was a little bit of diffidence as we prepared to tear out the first pew. But Les Black, a burly ex-navy man, stepped forward and heaved away a massive pew and with a groan it broke away from the wooden floor, and it was carried out to the waiting lorry. It wasn't an easy task for those who had had long associations with the church, but we all knew that it was a job that had to be done. There could be no progress without the removal of the old.

It wasn't a popular act with some people whose connections with the church were more sentimental than real. As the pews were stacked on top of the lorry parked in the Market Square, passers-by gawked at what we were doing and gasped at the apparent destruction that was going on in the church. It must have seemed a gross act of vandalism as cherished symbols of the Christian faith were taken away. 'Sacrilege!' cried a man to Tony as he and a few others staggered out with the Holy Communion table. 'How could they do this to our church!' As the man was totally unknown to us all, we could only guess that his links with the church ceased years before.

But we had great support from the civic authorities. Over the year we had developed harmonious and close working relationships with them, and the chief executive was clearly on our side—delighted that the civic church was actually attempting to do something which had social consequences. As a result, when we asked if we could use the Town Hall for Sunday worship while we were out of our building, they were only too pleased to put it at our disposal for a reasonable hire charge.

It was a strange experience worshipping in the Town Hall. This building was situated in the Square only thirty yards away from the church we were vacating. The big hall was almost the same size as the church, and it had a smaller hall adjoining, which was ideal for our Sunday School. The interior of the hall was decorated with plaques commemorating mayors and aldermen of Durham, together with former bishops and other dignitaries of note. Smiling down on us, and in some cases scowling, were pictures of long dead earls and dukes, bishops and other local worthies. To brighten up the place we imported some of our banners which proclaimed 'Jesus is Lord' or some other Christian affirmation.

Our first Sunday morning in the Town Hall was a thrilling and momentous occasion. We were psychologically aware in this first service of the self-imposed exile we had chosen. We were a congregation without a church building and we did not have the security that a building brings. It was a marvellous opportunity to begin to discover what a church really is, without the potential idolatry of a religious building. David Day, one of our lay leaders, spoke very movingly of the challenge before us. Preaching on 1 Chronicles 29:6 he drew out the themes of our poverty, mortality and frailty: 'We have lost our church for a time,' he said, 'but our security was never there anyway. We are going to trust in God.'

The first lesson we received from worshipping in the Town Hall was perhaps the most significant of all. We started our pattern of worship by facing the stage. I and my colleagues took the service from the stage at the end of the hall with the congregation facing us, stretching out to the back.

After three weeks of this pattern, one of the church wardens echoed my feelings. 'It's not working, is it? Somehow we seem more churchy here than we ever were in the church.' I agreed with this. 'Yes, we are trying to be a church in a secular building and we are finding it incongruous. We need to be more adventurous. What can we do?'

We eventually decided to swing the congregation round to face one of the longer walls and we placed the table and seats for the ministers in the middle so that the congregation were facing us on three sides. It was a splendid success. It increased our sense of fellowship enormously because we could now see one another instead of backs of heads. Our awareness of being the body of Christ improved greatly by this simple act. To our pleasure also we discovered that this step was appreciated by many of our older folk. One lady in her eighties said to me that it was a wonderful thing to be able to see other Christians and to feel that we belonged together.

But we were challenged by the secular building in another way. Because the building was so clearly unecclesiastical, it made it easier for non-churchgoers to feel part of the fellowship. As streams of people made their way into the Town Hall on Sunday mornings and evenings, so others, curious to know what was going on, were drawn along as well. Many came out of interest to find out why the Town Hall was packed on a Sunday. Some, of course, soon beat a hasty retreat when they found themselves in a service of worship, but others stayed and joined in and found themselves actually enjoying Christian worship! This was again a salutary lesson for us and gave us an increasing consciousness of the existence of the wider community. Archbishop Temple's memorable statement that 'Christianity is the only organization that exists for the benefit of those who are not its members' is not always at the forefront of the church's attention, but worshipping in the Town Hall certainly kept it at the front of ours.

As well as letting us have access to their premises, the city council showed their generosity in another way. The chief executive suggested to us in a private aside that the council might be sympathetic to the needs of the church if we made an application for financial help. This we did and, to our great surprise and joy, we were given an interest-free loan of £22,000! It is comparatively rare for a Christian group to be helped in this way because of a town council's policy to be impartial. But because of the special links between the council and the parish church, which go back hundreds of years, we were treated as a special case. 'We think your church is doing a splendid job in the city,' said Col. Miller. 'It is a mark of our appreciation.'

This generous act was in ironic contrast with our application to the Church Commissioners. After long negotiations, the Church Commissioners agreed to give us a similar loan. We thought at first that it was going to be on the same terms as the city loan, but to our dismay we found out that the Church Commissioners wanted 14% interest. To some of our folk who had no idea of the working of the inner life of the Church of England, it seemed disappointing that a secular body could give us an extraordinarily generous interest-free loan, but our own church which had given its blessings on our imaginative endeavours made sure that very little in fact was given away.

Into this exciting and changing situation a new curate arrived. A few months before we had said farewell to Pete and Sarah Broadbent. They had been excellent colleagues and friends. Pete's long hair and left-wing political views had been at first disconcerting to some, but everyone in the congregation appreciated his friendship and gifts. Frank White came from the same college as Pete and arrived to become the only churchless curate in the Church of England. I felt quite sorry for Frank in his first service at the Town Hall. After the splendid ordination service in the Norman Cathedral in the morning, the Town Hall must have seemed an astonishing contrast. But Frank took all this in his stride. He revelled in the unusual nature of his curacy and before a week was out he was truly in his element. Frank's great gift was his pastoral ability. He had an easy natural way with people and his love for them came across in a genuine and accepting manner. Because he was from the North-East, he was very much at home with Geordies.

Frank's own spiritual development connected with the way the church was developing. He had been brought up as a Roman Catholic, and his devout family were heartbroken when he rejected Catholicism in his teens. At university while studying social sciences he met up with the Christian Union and became a committed Christian. Eventually he was led to offer himself for ministry within the Church of England and to follow a call to ministry which was to lead him to Durham, only twelve miles from his home. Although his spiritual wanderings appeared at first to take him a long way from the faith of his parents and his brother Mark, who eventually became a Catholic priest, he was led towards them again through the reality of his faith in Christ. It was wonderful to see Frank's family with him at his ordination.

Indeed, a mark of our fellowship and worship was a love for fellow Christians, regardless of denominations. I could never fence the table of Holy Communion off from baptized Christians of other denominations, and we used to declare that if people loved Christ and wanted to serve him, then they were welcome to join us in this fellowship meal. We began to find that Roman Catholic Christians were among our congregation and felt part of our life. We then had to work through the question: to what extent were we to allow doctrinal differences to intrude in our relationships with those who came to us? I felt instinctively that a doctrinal 'means test' to distinguish 'sound' from 'unsound' Christians was unwise. We were of course very aware of the different doctrinal confessions of the denominations, but we believed that if a church is clear in its teaching and faithful to the Scriptures, the Holy Spirit will work in the lives of individuals and apply such doctrinal tests as he wants applied. We need not do it ourselves. If Catholics found that they could not square our teaching with that of their Church, then it was between them and the Lord to decide what action should be taken. We did not feel it our task to 'come on heavy'. We were indeed finding the love of Christ drawing us together.

As well as finding Catholic Christians among our fellowship, it was a fact that in the North-East some remarkable things were happening among Catholic congregations. In Durham we had the most cordial relationships with Fr Tweedy and his congregation at St Cuthbert's. But wherever I and our team went in the North-East leading weekend conferences and celebration services we would meet up with Catholic Christians and find a sense of expectancy among them. On one occasion we led a conference at Washington Ecumenical Centre on the themes of worship and evangelism. I asked the organizer to tell me what denominations would be represented.

'Oh, there will be quite a few denominations represented today,' he said, 'but the largest group will be the Catholics. You will easily recognize them—they will be the keen evangelical types!' As I had never heard the term 'evangelical' used of a Catholic I looked forward with great interest to my first encounter with one. And to my pleasure, it was as the organizer had said. The Catholics stood out by their enthusiasm and zeal and seemed more anxious than any other group to relate their faith to life. This impression was reinforced by other conferences I led. There appeared to be a great longing on the part of rank-and-file Catholics to renew their church.

The other side of the coin was that the Roman Catholic establishment frustrated the attempts made by many Catholics to bring about change. Although there were some priests who clearly saw that charismatic Christianity had something to offer, there were many who were frightened in case the church drifted away from its traditions. Our own role therefore as a bridge church in Durham was particularly important because we were able to support Christians of other denominations who, for the moment, could not get the same fellowship and teaching within their own denomination.

While we were in the Town Hall, a disastrous split occurred in the Durham churches, which was upsetting to many of us because it harmed the harmonious inter-church bond that had grown up. A group of young Christians from a number of other fellowships felt a strong call from God to establish a house church. Their reason for doing so was twofold. First, they felt that the established churches were not doing enough to reach non-churchgoers. Second, they wanted freedom for charismatic worship and found the structures of the churches in Durham too restricting. As a result about a hundred Christians, mainly students, left other churches to form the new body. As a congregation we were largely unaffected. We had cause to thank God for the unity in our own fellowship which meant that none of our local congregation were tempted to join, and only a few of our students left us to go to this church, which was to be called Emmanuel House Church.

I was strongly opposed to the formation of this new group because it represented yet another tragic rupture in the already torn body of Christ. It also seemed to be totally unnecessary. I pleaded with the leaders of Emmanuel not to break away, pointing out that, as far as I was aware, the New Testament only gave one reason for separation—and that is, separation on the basis of heresy. In this case no doctrinal conflict existed. Instead the formation of the church appeared to stem from desire to start a church which would be completely under the control of the Spirit, unrestricted from the bonds of tradition and man-made laws. How many groups in history have had that desire! But history has taught that breaking away from the historical church is not the way to put things right.

I was deeply disturbed by the hurt and distress it caused the Rev. Stephen Davis of St Margaret's, who had been a pioneering leader of the charismatic movement in Durham. Through his ministry great things had happened, and now he was brought very low through this new fellowship which was taking away some of his leaders. As a result it weakened his church and damaged his ministry as well as that of Claypath United Reformed Church.

Our pleas and arguments went unheeded and Emmanuel Church began its life. At that point we at St Nic's felt now it was established we should not remain in a spirit of antagonism, but should try to be a bridge church to help to heal the conflict. We therefore invited the leaders of Emmanuel to meet up with us monthly to pray together and to explore ways of co-operation. It was right, we thought, to extend an olive branch and do all we could to repair the damage caused.

One issue that continued to separate the house church from us was their practice of rebaptism. As we were meeting regularly with the leaders we were able to talk this over frankly, but we were not able to reach a common mind. It is very natural for young Christians who have had a spiritual experience to want to celebrate it in a public act. Many of them who experienced the Holy Spirit in a deeper way through what some call the 'baptism of the Spirit', and what I prefer to call 'renewal in the Spirit', asked for baptism. The house church therefore hired the public baths every now and then to have mass baptism. The problems began when it became evident that people were being rebaptized. Some of the folk who were baptized came from Christian homes and had been offered to the Lord at their birth. Such rebaptisms raised acute problems for the other churches as they saw this new body cheerfully disregarding earlier baptism.

The problem of baptism is, of course, a delicate and painful issue which has long been a cause of separation between Christians. Evangelicals find themselves on opposite sides of the fence on this matter. While being fully at one on essentials such as the person and work of Christ, most will admit that Scripture itself is not clear on the matter of infant baptism. While it is true that believers' baptism was the norm in the first century, it is clear that Christians started to baptize their young soon after the New Testament period. They had to consider, as we do, the place of a believer's child in the covenant relationship that exists between God and his people. The evidence therefore is ambiguous. We certainly did not want this issue to separate us from other Christians because there are so many more important doctrines for us to preach about and share with the world. Nevertheless, our own policy at that time was that we would decline to rebaptize Christians. In the case of young Christians requesting baptism we would see this as a teaching opportunity to explain the meaning of baptism. The most difficult cases were those who came from non-Christian homes and who were probably 'christened' as children because it was the done thing. Nevertheless, I argued, we should not deny that symbol however imperfectly understood. In the case of infant baptism, I would continue, baptism always anticipated the arrival of personal response. In the Church of England, this is expressed in Confirmation. In the case of students who felt that they must express their new faith publicly, we would feed them into confirmation classes; or, if they had already been confirmed, give them an opportunity to give their testimony and reaffirm their baptismal vows. But it must be said that it was never a major issue with us, even though it had become a problem in other Durham churches.

But we did have a marvellous and unforgettable baptism soon after we moved into the Town Hall. Simon, a postgraduate student, came to see Frank and asked to be baptized. He wanted, he said, to be baptized in the River Wear. As it was the middle of November, we pointed out that it wasn't the time to enter the Wear. But he was adamant, and we agreed. So, towards the end of the family service, the congregation trooped down to the river and I led a short service while my colleague Frank waded into the river with Simon and baptized him. I most certainly had the more comfortable part taking the service from the bank! The amusing thing was that Frank could not swim an inch, so under his track suit he had a life jacket and a rope tied to his waist. But he need not have worried— Simon was an experienced life-saver! As well as being a great experience for Simon it was a great moment for the church as we streamed out of the Town Hall and crowded the banks. Curious passers-by watched from the bridge and banks as we sang and as Simon expressed his faith in Christ in this powerful symbol of Christian believing.

Just before Christmas 1980, my colleague Mark Townson came to see me. Once again he asked for permission to erect his shanty hut outside the church. Then he suddenly asked 'Is it possible to get married on Christmas Day?' Thinking that this was a fairly general question similar to, 'Is the moon made of green cheese?' I replied, 'Yes, of course you can.'

'In that case,' he said, 'Sue and I want you to marry us on Christmas Day in St Nic's. Will you do it?'

'Mark,' I gasped, 'you've left it a bit late, haven't you? There are not enough Sundays now for the publishing of Banns of marriage, and in case you haven't noticed, we haven't got a church. It is completely unusable!'

'I know,' he said coolly, 'but we have looked into this and we know that we can get the Archbishop's licence to marry. As for the church, yes, we want to be married in our church, whatever its condition.'

'But what about the congregation?' I asked. 'They will want to be there. They have a great affection for you.'

He shifted uncomfortably at this and said, 'Sue and I don't want a fuss. It doesn't go with our life style to have a traditional wedding with lots of presents. All we want is you to take the service with a few friends like Alison, Frank and Eileen. We don't want a reception or anything like that.'

Eventually I agreed to marry them as requested on Christmas Day, and Eileen volunteered to put on a reception afterwards in the vicarage, for them, their parents and the few friends and relatives who were in on the secret.

Before we could have the wedding we had to make the church as presentable as possible. So a few of us went down to see what condition the church was in. It was the first time I had been back to the building since we took the pews out, and the place looked just like a bomb site. The floor was up, and rubble, broken concrete and dirt were everywhere. A small bulldozer stood in the middle of the church. Planks formed bridges over deep trenches in the floor that were eventually going to be part of the new heating system. As I stood there looking at this devastation I felt very depressed. 'Oh God,' I thought, 'What have I done to this place? A place of worship for hundreds of years, and during my time it has been torn apart. Oh Lord, I don't want to go down in the history of this church as the vicar who destroyed it!'

Although I knew very well that the church needed drastic change and that God would provide for the completion of the building, the shock of seeing the building in that condition prompted this momentary feeling of gloom.

After lunch on Christmas Day, unbeknown to the rest of the congregation, eighteen of us met in derelict St Nic's to witness the marriage of Mark and Sue. Mark had ended his shanty hut vigil on Christmas Eve and looked a little gaunt and wan. Sue beside him, dressed in white, looked a radiant bride.

Frank and Alison had placed some benches in the sanctuary, and around us piercing the gloom were a dozen candles or so. The marriage was a beautiful and moving service and I drew a rather unlikely parallel between the church and their new relationship. 'Although we meet in this building which seems so dead and lifeless, it witnesses to a congregation which believes in the resurrection of Jesus. For that reason we have nailed our colours to the mast and have left the security of this place in order to discover a new future in God. We know that this church will be transformed and made new. We look around and see the reality of death, but by faith we see God's promises. Christmas is like that too. Who could have believed at the time that Jesus, a baby, could be God's chosen one? Hardly an auspicious beginning. But he was God's promise to mankind—a promise of life and hope. Today your marriage signals not the formed reality of your relationship and your love, but the promise of God's blessings on you.'

Following the marriage we sang the song 'The light of Christ has come into the world', and in the flickering candlelight the words came across with deeper meaning and significance. In the coldness and emptiness of the church that afternoon I caught a fresh glimpse of the reality of God's promises to us. Somehow I knew that everything was going to turn out perfectly.

As we entered 1981, we were conscious as a congregation that this year was going to be a year of fulfilment. Before the year was out we would be back in a transformed church building and we would know once and for all if our faith in God was a reality or a crass example of cloud-cuckoo-land living. But one thing we were sure of—we had to keep the spiritual challenge before the congregation. It is all too easy for Christians to slip back into inertia; we had to make sure we did not slide into complacency and slumber.

We therefore decided that on February 1st, instead of the clergy preaching at the three services, members of the Church Council would take them and challenge the congregation for renewed commitment. A group of us produced a document which we entitled 'Targets for Church Growth'. The document challenged each of us to pledge four things. First, that as individuals we should set aside time for private prayer and Bible reading. Second, that as a church we ought to commit ourselves to the house groups and to the prayer evenings. Our fellowship together was vitally important. Third, that further sacrificial giving was necessary if we wished to finish the project. Finally, that our attention should not only be on what we must do at home, but that our missionary interest and giving ought to increase. We therefore pledged £7,500 to a missionary project in Burundi.

The lay folk who led these services spoke with great conviction and power. As I listened to them relating their own faith to the needs of the church, and as they challenged us all, I marvelled at their spiritual maturity and ability. God had truly unleashed the talents of the congregation and, for me and my colleagues, it was a truly humbling and enriching experience to serve the servants of God and to see them develop to such a degree. Here I realized afresh that the secret of growth in any congregation is the congregation itself. If the gifts and talents of the people are not released, there can be no real progress. We could indeed praise God that many of the gifts of the Holy Spirit were operational in the congregation and harnessed by him in loving and united service.

13

Lessons of Faith

In 1 Kings there is the story of the step of faith that Elijah asked the widow of Zarephath to take. Because of the famine she was down to her last meal, when the prophet unexpectedly turned up and asked to share it. 'It's all we have left,' she protested. 'After this my son and I will die.'

'I promise you this,' Elijah said, 'if you let me share with you, your bowl will never run out of flour and your cruse of oil will never run dry.' We are told that she took the gamble and God's promise was fulfilled.

We have to admit that this is one of those Bible stories which take a bit of believing in our hard-headed and rational society. Even Christians find themselves saying at times: 'Go on, pull the other one!'

But God is like that. He is the provider and meets our need, even if he doesn't always work in quite so miraculous a way today.

During our period of exile in the Town Hall we too experienced the amazing goodness of the Lord. Like the widow we knew the risks involved. Before we took the plunge and signed the contract with the builders we had been told the score plainly. We half expected to be badly in debt six months after the start of the project, living dangerously on the brink of ruin and collapse. But the amazing thing is—it never happened! Never at any time were we in debt or in serious shortage of money. Even though the work had begun in the church and we were paying bills out, we always had enough. The cruse of oil, in our case, never ran dry.

On March 15th we had another Gift Day and £27,400 was given, including loans, bringing the gross fund to £207,000. This was less than a year since our first Gift Day, and it was a staggering and almost unbelievable total. Very little money had been obtained from outside the fellowship of the church. We had tried the Department of the Environment and had contacted many Trusts and firms—all without success. We knew that the majority of the money had to come from the congregation, but the way they kept responding was a vivid reminder of Elijah and the widow. Our bowl was not running out either. Surely, we often said to one another, this is a sign of God's goodness to us.

On that Gift Day my mind floated back nearly a year to the member of the congregation who refused to join the fund-raising group because, he said, raising £150,000 was impossible. The old Adam in me wanted to take his letter round to him and say, 'Do you remember writing this? It's impossible to raise £150,000, is it? Who's right, eh?' But respect for him stopped me from wanting to rub his nose in it. That man was probably more conscious than anyone else that he had been confounded by God's wonderful answers to our prayers.

Then later, on June 21st, another Gift Day was held and a further £21,500 was given, bringing our gross fund to £232,000. No wonder at the end of that day with a full heart we were able to sing:

> The steadfast love of the Lord never ceases,
> His mercies never come to an end,
> They are new every morning, new every morning,

Great is thy faithfulness to me, great is thy
faithfulness.

But at no point could we stop and gaze complacently at
what God was doing. We seemed to be on a moving
escalator which had no end. Not only was our giving
steadily moving up, but the disturbing thing was that the
target was moving too. From the 'guaranteed' figure of
£260,000, it went up to £275,000, then £290,000. We were
fearful in case the project went beyond £300,000. We
seemed to be chasing a moving object which was determined to elude us.

But through all this we were learning very important
lessons about God and about ourselves.

We were learning that God could be trusted. One man
said, 'I suppose I have always believed stories about God
in the Bible, but I don't think I really believed *in* the God
of the Bible. He always seemed to do amazing things back
there and never here in real life. What I have learned is
that God is the same. He does work today and we have
experienced his wonders among us.' Later David Day
preached a very helpful sermon on the problem of 'holy
history'. Wonderful things, he said, always happened back
there in the Bible or in Christian history or in other
people's lives, but never seemed to happen to us. But now
it was happening to us because God was invading our
situation, introducing the unexpected and the miraculous.

Because we were learning this lesson, to a considerable
degree fear was largely gone from the congregation. I was
conscious myself that, since the Council gave the go-ahead
the previous October, I had not had a moment's real worry.
Somehow God's peace had been given to us and we knew
he could be trusted.

We were also learning the radical nature of faith. We
were like swimmers completely out of depth, far from
land and with no tangible hope of getting ashore. All you

can do in that kind of situation is to abandon yourself to God's will. This is, of course, one of the most difficult things for modern people to do. We like to have our security. I have found in my experience that clergy are among the most reluctant to cash out their faith when the chips are down.

'Faith,' said Dr Ian Ramsey, the former Bishop of Durham, 'is precisely the ability to live with uncertainty.' The uncertainty, of course, is not in God, but in us. We love to be sure and we don't want to follow God if it means that we have to be kept in the dark, as it were. Even mature Christians can be like children clinging onto the sides in the shallows of a swimming pool splashing with their feet and crying, 'Look! I'm swimming!' But faith, if it is to be Christian faith, will contain risk, not knowing what precisely the outcome will be, leaving that to God.

We too were learning this. Our prayer and praise evenings continued, as did our half-nights of prayer, and we valued these times of fellowship and refreshment. They helped us to interpret what was going on and re-assured us that God was leading us further and further away from our resources into his. In one of his books, the German theologian Moltmann has a fine passage about Abraham's faith. 'He trusted in the word of promise more than all the security of his life beyond the river. He left the familiar patterns of his life which had provided a home and security for him. He abandoned his fatherland and became an alien. He left his friends and was alone. He left his father's house and lost his identity. He left even his gods....'

We were also discovering God's resources in one another. I was deeply touched when people gave things that were very precious to them. One day a student who was a gifted musician came to see me and offered his violin for the project. 'It's the most important thing I have,' he said, 'but I want to give it to God's work.'

One day I went to the front door to find a bulky envelope on the mat. In it was £400 from an old-age pensioner who had been left some money. In it was a note, 'A thanksgiving for the church which has meant so much to me. This is given that others may share the faith that has helped me.'

Perhaps I was most moved by the thirteen-year-old boy who had about £350 in his savings, and after talking with his parents came to see me because he wanted to loan it to the church free of interest, and as long as we liked! It was times like these that showed me that sacrificial giving was running very deep in the congregation. People were diverting money into the building project from savings, holidays, life insurances and so on. All this indicated that our giving had passed from generosity to surrender of our possessions.

Our own contribution to the project took the form of doing Bed and Breakfast for tourists in Durham. We had a seven bedroomed vicarage and we were able to reserve two large rooms for this task. This was Eileen's private empire mainly, and over three years she entertained nearly one thousand visitors and was able to give over £4,000 to the project. This added considerably to the pressure of life at the vicarage, what with constant church meetings as well, but it was well worth the trouble.

A third factor we were learning was about our own weakness. As winter passed into spring and spring into summer, we were all becoming very tired. Tired of Gift Days, tired of countless meetings to do with the building, let alone the ongoing activities of normal church life. We were so very tired of the effort involved in getting the Town Hall ready for worship. Every Sunday a team of people had to make the hall ready for worship and then put things away at the end of the day. It was a weary and wearing business and we longed to be free of it. From another perspective it was very good for us all. We had to pull together. We couldn't just leave things to only the church wardens and a few old faithfuls; we had to pool our resources and give our time and talents. The result was that commitment to one another in the congregation was very deep indeed. This showed in the way people cared for one another—they were observant of the needs of others and a caring attitude grew.

And the congregation was growing as well. This was certainly not the case of a project totally controlling the resources of a congregation. Our normal organizations were growing and people were coming into the life of the church and to a deeper faith in Christ. One man who had little contact with the Christian church since boyhood came to worship with us out of curiosity. He told me at the door of the Town Hall after a service, 'I came along to see the church where everyone has to queue to get in!'

'What did you make of the service? Did you like it?' I asked. 'It was OK,' he said cautiously, 'but I think you'll see me again.' And we did. He gradually wormed his way into the life of the church and quietly slipped into the community of faith. He was typical of many men who joined the congregation. Not for them the sudden bolt of conversion, but rather the gradual, cautious acceptance of the Christian faith as God's Spirit worked quietly within them.

At the end of a long Council meeting in the vicarage I received a telephone call which was to have the most unexpected repercussions on the vicarage family. It was from Trinity College, Bristol, a theological college which trained men and women for Christian ministry. 'George,' said the spokesman at the other end, 'you probably know that we are looking for a Principal. Have you thought of applying?'

'Certainly not!' I said, 'we are very happy here. How can we possibly think of moving when we are in the middle of a building project? It would be an act of betrayal to think of moving this year.' After thanking the caller for thinking of us for that role, I put the phone down thinking that was the end of that.

But it wasn't. Other phone calls and letters from Bristol and elsewhere followed. We made it clear as patiently as we could that we could not contemplate another post at this stage. But another telephone call from another council member of Trinity College made us hesitate. 'George,' said Paul Berg, Vicar of the important church of Christ Church, Clifton, in Bristol, 'a number of us believe that you may be the right person for us here. Now we respect that you cannot come this year because of the project, but would you be prepared to meet the council and at least consider the possibility that it might be right?'

'No, Paul,' I replied, 'I have made our position very plain. It is impossible just yet. I cannot and will not consider it.' I put the phone down and Eileen looked at me in a troubled way; 'How can we be sure that it is right to stay on once the project is completed? Perhaps God is telling us to pack our bags.'

We decided to put down a 'fleece' as Gideon did in the book of Joshua. We decided that if any further letters came the following day we would consider it carefully, if unhappily. We went to bed feeling quite secure that no such confirmation would occur. The following day two letters came from Bristol urging us to consider applying for this post at Trinity College. We very reluctantly decided to meet the council, and we accepted the post on condition that we would not move from Durham for fifteen months until the project was well and truly behind us.

For a time we were very confused by this sudden change of direction. Why was it that we were being told to move on before the project was completed? Most of our time at St Nicholas's had been spent building up the congregation, making many changes and engaging in this drastic building scheme. And now God was tapping us on the shoulder saying, 'Your time is up. Off you go, folks.' We wouldn't even have any time to enjoy the new facilities and shape its future ministry!

It was therefore with a very heavy heart that at our Annual General Meeting in 1981 I had to announce that in July 1982 we would be moving on. It was very hard for the congregation to take this halfway through the project, but it made us all the more aware that it rested not on our labours or human personalities, but on God himself. A very dear friend wrote, 'God is taking you both away because it is his work and not yours, your job is done and his continues.' This was obviously something we had to accept even though it was hard to take. Perhaps no congregation has ever meant as much as the fellowship of St Nicholas's, and it was a separation we were not looking forward to.

We were also learning the lesson of being a fellowship of the Holy Spirit. A community of the Spirit is expectant and open to new possibilities, and we were beginning to allow him his way among us. It is true that we were not as open as I would have liked. I longed for us to experience together more of the gifts of the Spirit that the New Testament speaks of, but God restrained my impatience and he was working in the body gently building us up and encouraging the flowering of his gifts. The fruit of the Spirit was very clearly noticeable among us. Through prayer and the deeper level of commitment brought about by the project, the former critical spirit which had provoked many of the controversies about worship was completely gone. No longer was our worship hampered by tension. There was now a real spirit of freedom and joy and acceptance of one another.

There was also a lovely atmosphere among those who attended the 9.00 a.m. service which had a more traditional style of worship. Many of the regulars at this service had been critical of the building scheme when it was first suggested, but they remained in the fellowship and gave their loyal support. Here too we were conscious that the Holy Spirit's peace prevailed.

But the keynote of spiritual fellowship is the centrality of Jesus. Although the Spirit gives us his gifts his main role is to point us to Christ. He 'glorifies' Christ—this is the biblical teaching. This was happening among us in a variety of different ways; through the lives of Christians, through our Watersports activity, and through the preaching. But I was getting more excited by the fact that members of the congregation were now beginning to talk about their faith openly, and as a result of this they were bringing their friends along to the Town Hall for worship. They were no longer embarrassed about advertising Sunday worship. It was tremendously encouraging to see this happening.

'I'm not a churchgoer,' explained one man, 'but I've been impressed by what Jim has told me about his faith and his church and I have come along to see what was going on.'

This reply interested me greatly because it showed the important link between a person's faith and the Christian community he comes from. My reading of the New Testament suggests that the early Christians never went out just telling what Jesus meant to them personally. They would not have separated their faith from that of their fellowship. To say 'Jesus is Lord', which was most probably the earliest Christian confession, joined them to a church where his lordship was acknowledged. To be 'in Christ' and to be 'in the church' is synonymous in the New Testament. I was therefore very pleased that our Christians were beginning to link together the doctrine of Christ and the doctrine of the church. They were going into their work situations, colleges, schools and homes with a story that was a community experience. They were able then to talk in a natural way about the church and their place in it.

One man recounted an amusing incident at work, when the day after one of our Gift Days the men in his office were talking about their recreation the previous day. One had been fishing and told of his successes. My friend said casually, 'Well, we had a remarkable day yesterday as well. I go to St Nicholas's Church—you know, the one in the Market Square. Do you know how much money we got in the collection? £27,000!'

'Go on!' exclaimed the fisherman, 'have you got millionaires there?'

'Pennies from heaven—or more likely tenners from heaven,' joked another.

'No, we have ordinary people who believe in something very much. We are raising this money because....' In that way he was able to talk about his faith because it was a common experience he could refer to, which was verifiable.

This realization that we were sharing a corporate experience of faith in Christ, and that we were beginning to work from this base in evangelism and service, was a heartening thing. All this was coming about in the context of the Spirit's work among us, deepening our understanding and appreciation of the body. One of our leaders said of his own experience of renewal: 'Our experience has been a gradual opening of our eyes to a new dimension of spiritual experience—the Holy Spirit taking his true place in the Trinity and in our experience.'

14

What—No Pews?

The Bishop of Durham stood in the middle of the church and looked around critically at the progress of the builders. He had just taken a Confirmation service for us in the Town Hall and he had asked to see the current state of the work. I warned him that it was far from complete, but this did not deter him—he would still like to see it, he said. There was little doubt that he was impressed. Even though there was still structural work to be done, furnishings to go in and carpets to be laid—to say nothing of decoration —the potential of the building showed through.

'It's splendid!' he said, 'the congregation must be very pleased with what has been achieved. I do hope it will be a building that will be greatly used for the kingdom of God. I am looking forward to seeing it in its finished state in October.'

We were not quite as pleased as the Bishop. The progress was not as quick as we would like. The opening of the church was planned for October 23rd, to be followed by ten days of celebration, and we could see trouble brewing if the builders did not get a move on.

This fear was confirmed in July when the architect informed us that the work on the main church area would not to be completed until October 10th. We then needed fourteen days following that for the installation of the organ, furnishings and the laying of the carpet. To make matters worse, we could not get into the halls to decorate them until the builders had made good the plaster. The earliest we could decorate the halls was the middle of September.

Once again there was very little we could do about this except to put as much pressure on the architect as we possibly could. John Ledger, chairman of the project committee, had a crucial role at this time. He spent hours on the phone maintaining contact with architect and builders to make sure that the momentum was sustained.

Apart from that, all we could do was to leave the difficulty with God. In fact, God seemed to be thumping this point home again and again: 'I am to be trusted. Leave it with me. Don't worry.' Our natural inclination is to worry, but somehow God was getting through to us at last. In one of my sermons at the time I referred to God as Master of 'cliff-hanging situations'. He may keep us dangling until the minute before midnight, but he always comes in time. How true this had been of our experience time and again. Once again, we had to trust him with the unknown.

As soon as we were able, we got into the halls to decorate them from top to bottom. The congregation turned out splendidly to take their part in this activity. Men, women, teenagers and youngsters came along to give a hand. The halls were in a terrible condition and the upper one especially had not been done for years. It took weeks of hard work because everything had to be stripped right down, including the floors which had to be sanded and then resealed. It was hard and messy, but it was an important part of our spiritual activity too. It was a symbolic offering of ourselves in a physical way. We had given our minds to the Lord in planning the scheme, we had given our money sacrificially to pay for it, and now many of us were giving to God and his building our physical labour of love.

As autumn approached, our concern deepened that the buildings would not be completed in time, and the architect reinforced this worry by telling us that the builders were behind schedule yet again. Surely it was asking too much of God to pull off this cliff-hanger!

To add to our concern, we were also told that the projected cost of the building was £310,000. Our gross fund stood well short of the target, at £238,500. My earlier fears were now realized. The cost was well over £300,000 and still rising. Could the congregation raise yet another £72,000 on top of the amazing sacrifices that had already been made? Humanly speaking it seemed improbable, but we had lived with the improbable for so long that all we could do was to take a deep breath and hold on. Frank White in a talk at one of our prayer evenings said, 'In Scripture, God often allows dark situations to get darker in order to show the wonder of his might—our situation is an opportunity for us to stand and "see the salvation of our God".'

The last ten days before the opening of the church were days of frenetic activity in the building. Builders, painters, joiners, electricians and others jostled with one another as they endeavoured to get the church ready. Into this confusion came carpet layers, sound installation people, people with kitchen fittings, the organ builder and his team.

As it seemed so desperate and confused, we decided to have a church 'pray-in'. Other people have 'sit-ins' we thought, why not a pray-in, to dedicate every aspect of the place to him? It was a kind of 'prayer occupation' of the church to make it and us spiritually ready for the task of service ahead. About fifty of us therefore met ten days before the opening to commit the future of the church to God.

For some people the new church was completely staggering. They hadn't been back since they left the church thirteen months previously, and now they stood there gazing open-mouthed at the building, even though there was still much to be done.

'Isn't it beautiful!' the exclamation came from an elderly lady who had been critical of the project from the start. But she had been faithful in her support in prayer and now she was completely won over. We were all dumbfounded by the transformation of the building. It was so much better than we dreamed possible. The place was warm, light and welcoming. The roof was attractively and brightly decorated in traditional medieval colours of pink, white and green. Everything seemed to blend together into a most attractive combination of old and new. The new screen with the large wrought-iron cross made a marvellous focal point and matched the new gallery alongside splendidly.

We broke into small groups and, like small children at their first party, gaped at the splendour all around. As Eileen and I looked, our minds floated back to Christmas Day when Mark and Sue were married. We recalled the total devastation of the building and our feelings of despair. And here we were, standing in the same place dazzled by a scheme brought about by the faith of a congregation which had the temerity to believe in a God who worked today. Our hearts were crying with the psalmist, 'Bless the Lord, O my soul, and forget not all his benefits.' His benefits were all around for us to see.

After our exploration of the building we started our pray-in. We went first to the entrance with the symbol of the 'fish' which was the first thing people would see as they entered the church from the Market Place. The fish symbol was a secret sign of the early Christians in times of persecution and signifies 'Jesus Christ, Son of God, Saviour'. And we prayed that many who entered the church would one day believe in him and find him to be the way, the truth and the life.

Then we assembled in the welcome area with the Christian book display and prayed that those who entered would find a welcome here and that none would be turned away. And again, my mind flashed back to that tramp who left notes for me on the Holy Table and I thought of many others who had come into this place looking for counsel and help, only to find it unattended. 'Never again,' I thought, 'will the church be left unmanned. It will be open to all and there will be someone here to welcome them and help if needed.'

And then we moved to the shop tucked away in the corner near the main road. The shop had grown out of Richard's Saturday shop and we prayed for him and all who would serve in it, that it would truly be a community shop and help the disadvantaged, providing a bridge into the church family.

And so we went around each place in the building, praying over its ministry for God—the quiet chapel, the kitchen, the organ, the historical display, the halls. And then with quiet thankfulness we left the building, excited by the promise we had seen and humbled that God had chosen us to be part of this work.

The Opening Day arrived. Frantic workmen were still putting finishing touches to the building right up to the Bishop's entrance. The actual service had been prepared by my former colleague, Pete Broadbent, who had imaginatively combined the notes of thanksgiving, celebration and dedication in the liturgy. With some regret we had to restrict the service to the congregation and friends who had supported us over the years previously. There were many local people who wanted to be there for the opening, but it was only right that the service of dedication should be for the church family. There was no room for anyone else—the place was packed with the local congre-

gation and former members who had left the district but
had returned for this great occasion.

Three of us gave brief talks in the service. Geoff Moore,
Church Warden, spoke on behalf of the congregation and
gave a short description of the vision which had led us on.
John Ledger as Chairman of the project struck a note of
commitment: 'Today is only a beginning of a new era for
St Nicholas's Church,' he said. 'The building is only a
means to an end. It is you—the living stones—who are the
spiritual house of God. You can use this building with all
its facilities to make the Christian faith meaningful to
people in Durham and all who pass by.'

This was similar to the emphasis I made. I had long
been impressed by the title of a book about Mother Teresa
called *Something Beautiful for God*. 'We have renovated
an old and dreary building which handicapped God's
work,' I said, 'and we have made it beautiful, flexible and
usable. It is beautiful for God. It is not for ourselves or our
own comfort, but that others may find a living Lord and
find healing and wholeness in him. Once this project is
completed our work does not stop, it continues in a
different form. This building is beautiful for God so that
God's beauty can be known.'

Then the Bishop, led by myself and the wardens, did a
ceremonial walk around the church. The Bishop blessed
each part, while the music group led singing in between.
The Bishop obviously found the blessing of the shop
amusing, because when he had finished he remarked,
'I've done some strange things in my time, but this is the
first time I have ever dedicated and blessed a shop!'

In his sermon, the Bishop stressed the continuity
between the old and the new. 'On this spot Christians
have worshipped for hundreds of years,' he said, 'and
during that time they have had to adapt to new situations
and new challenges. The church that does not adapt is
sentenced to be a mysterious ghetto existing on the fringe

of society contributing nothing to its life. To live is to change, and a changing church is a sign of life within. In our service tonight we do not dedicate a new building, but an existing church for new ministries and new challenges.'

As the Bishop preached this stirring sermon on the link between the old and the new, I thought back to the ministries of those who had gone before. The Rev. George Marchant had spent over twenty years as vicar, and before him there were other godly incumbents and their congregations who had served God faithfully here. We were truly building on the inheritance of others and entering into their labours. The Bishop's sermon was a fitting reminder to us all that evening that in God's economy of salvation each one of us has our own part to play. Some of us have the hard task of picking out the stones from the field and know only discouragement and difficulty; others come along and plough the land and sow the seed; and at last others come along and reap the harvest. Wherever we come in the sequence the same task of faithfulness and obedience is required. God requires nothing more. It is *his* work to make something of it.

The opening service introduced ten days of celebration during which the church was at last open to all and manned daily. Films, lectures, meals and many other special events were held to show the flexibility of the building and to express the note of celebration. Sir Norman Anderson was one of our special speakers and he gave a lunchtime talk on the resurrection. About 200 people were in the church to hear Sir Norman, and his talk made a big impression on those who were there. One man who claimed to be an agnostic was deeply challenged by this talk and afterwards said to Sir Norman, 'I have always regarded the Christian idea of resurrection as a romantic, but improbable story. But you have shown me that I cannot dismiss it that easily. I am now going away to think it through more carefully.' He did, and over the weeks that followed he read the gospel accounts and a few books on the resurrection and perhaps surprised himself more than anyone else when be became a Christian!

During the ten days of celebration, hundreds of people came into the church each day to see over the new building as well as to take part in the special activities. There were a few who were plainly horrified by what they saw and some stamped out in fury, never sharing their anger with anyone. But the vast majority were pleased. 'What—no pews?' was the usual initial comment. But when it was explained that we had chosen chairs because they were more adaptable than pews, they left well pleased that a church was taking active steps to reach the world with the gospel of Christ.

One afternoon soon after the building was completed I got chatting with a man who was visiting Durham for the day. He explained that he was not an evangelical but was nevertheless deeply interested in what we were doing. I replied, 'We are not attempting to wave banners here, or draw attention to ourselves. We simply want to live out an attractive New Testament Christianity in order to help others find the Christ we know.'

'I see that,' he said, 'I think it shows in the combination of simplicity, adaptability, and attractive Christian symbolism. In one important way, this church and the Cathedral are alike!'

I was most interested to hear more about this because the two places were in my opinion very different. 'Oh no,' he said, 'when I go into the Cathedral and I stand there in that vast and majestic building it seems to say to me, "you are small and finite, but God is awesome and majestic, clothed in splendour and light," and I leave humbled, knowing that I am a creature of a great God. But as I wandered around your warm, brightly lit, much smaller building it seems to say, "You are loved and accepted, a member of God's family; he is your heavenly Father and wants you to enter into fellowship with him," and I leave encouraged knowing that he cares for me.' The man continued, taking a breath, 'These two things are not incompatible, you know. We need both emphases as Christians. That is why the Cathedral and St Nicholas's are alike. They are symbols of the transcendent, but in different ways.'

That was a helpful point of view and a reminder that no one church can possibly meet the spiritual needs of all people. There are going to be people whose way into the Christian faith will be through the kind of images of life provoked by places like the Cathedral. St Nicholas's with its warmth and informal style has its place within the wide spectrum of the Christian family and we must not worry if not every Christian is going to find it the most congenial place to worship.

As the church settled down, so we began to find that many ordinary people began to use it as a place of prayer. Because it is in the heart of the town it is seen as a natural place to pop in and spend a little time in prayer and meditation. Christians of all traditions, and people of none, came to use it as a place for prayer. During the weekdays we were able to screen off the sanctuary area to form a quiet chapel, and an active ministry of intercession started. A school exercise book was placed there together with a pen, and people were invited to write down prayer needs. Most moving petitions were entered into the book from people of all age groups. They were glad that the church was willing to share their needs with them.

But people came in for other reasons too—to rest, to visit the shop or just out of curiosity to see what was going on inside the graceful church building in the centre of the town. A professionally prepared display proclaimed the meaning of the Christian faith with leaflets for any who wanted to study it further. Hundreds of the leaflets were taken away and read during the first few weeks of opening.

One afternoon soon after the opening a group of teen-agers entered laughing and joking. 'Eh! Look at this—it's a church!' said one of the fellows with a mop of dyed hair. 'But it's modern,' said a girl. 'It's not like a normal church, is it? It's quite good, really,' she added grudgingly.

One of our young 'manners' approached and asked, 'Would you like me to show you over the church and explain what we have done?'

'Why not,' they agreed, and I overheard our 'manner' explaining the story. That evening they were back in the building for a special event for young people. The building had started its work to attract.

It was good to be back in our own building after the months of exile in the Town Hall. It had been a rich uplifting experience to be severed from a church building, and we had learned a great deal about fellowship and faith during that time. But it was a little like being a lodger in someone else's home and not having the freedom to do what we wanted. Now that we were back, we had the building seven days a week and could really use the place for the glory of God.

But in one significant way the Town Hall made its mark on us and our worship. The thought of worshipping in a traditional manner by facing the east, just seeing backs of heads, was clearly not for us as a rule. Although we felt there would be times when we would want to be tradi-tional, the general feeling was that we should continue worshipping 'in the round'. So we moved the staging in front of the fish by the entrance and arranged the chairs so that the congregation surrounded the table on three sides.

Our first Holy Communion in the building on our first Sunday was a deep, emotional experience for us all. We shared together the joy of being back home and we rejoiced in a God whose goodness is beyond our under-standing and whose timing is perfect. Indeed, we recalled the fact that all our deadlines had been reached. We may have been cliff hanging a little, but at no point had we fallen. That evening we echoed David's prayer at the building of the temple, 'O Lord, we have brought together all this wealth to build a temple to honour your name, but it all came from you and all belongs to you.' With a God like this we could trust him for the future.

15

Facing the Future

In a famous phrase the theologian Emil Brunner defined the nature of the church: 'As a fire exists by burning, so the church exists by mission.' A church does not exist for itself, but for the world.

Now that the church plant was renewed and the people of God were experiencing God's renewal, we had to keep before us the needs of society and our role in serving it and witnessing to God's love in Christ.

Ideally it seemed to me, this should take two forms. First, Christians should live out their faith in their jobs and in the community. A church should not absorb the attention and time of Christians to such a degree that they end up by having no time to get involved in trade union activities, local politics, community welfare work and so on. I was delighted to see a good number of the congregation making a contribution towards such organizations as Citizens Advice Bureau, Samaritans, Gingerbread, Cyrenians and prison welfare work. If Christians are to be 'salt' in society, the salt must get into what it is trying to preserve. It's of little use on its own.

Second, the church should take direct action in publicizing its life and message. Its basic purpose, as Brunner's phrase suggests, is to be a servant of its message. In our case, now that the project was behind us, the Council decided to plan and prepare for a relaxed and home-grown mission, which we called Open Doors, as a simple attempt to move away from the building into the homes of the community around. About fifty supper parties and other activities were organized in the week leading up to Palm Sunday. We had the help of three theological students and Denis Shepheard of the Church Pastoral Aid Society, but their role was not to dominate Open Doors, rather to assist the congregation. Families were urged to invite their friends, work colleagues and neighbours for a meal and to hear one of the congregation or clergy speak for ten minutes about 'what Easter means to me'. Leaflets about the Christian faith were available and people were also invited to the central events that were going on in the church that week.

We learned a great deal from this low-key activity. We discovered that non-churchgoing people are usually very grateful when Christians are able to share their faith with them, as long as it is done sensitively and lovingly. One man said to one of the congregation after a supper party: 'I've never been much of a churchgoer, but I have always been interested in Christianity. It has often puzzled me why churchgoers have never bothered to tell me about their faith like other people with deep beliefs. For that reason I found this evening very helpful indeed.' We were greatly encouraged that not only did we receive apprecia-tive comments about the activity itself, but that a handful of people became Christians, and others who had some distant connection with the church started to come to worship.

But I also observed that Christians are on the whole terrified of direct evangelism. In the weeks leading up to Open Doors many of the congregation were showing signs of disenchantment with the activity, even though I had gone out of my way to avoid the word 'mission' because of its overtones of 'let's go out and get them'. Why was it, I asked myself, that we can talk so freely and naturally about football, the weather, politics and the state of the economy, and yet feel so ill at ease when it comes to talking about something which means everything to us?

But that is precisely the problem, I realized. Because Christianity is so important to us, many are reluctant to talk about it—like a fragile plant that should not be exposed to the harsh challenge of the cold atmosphere outside. Some were clearly afraid of being confronted with difficult issues they could not answer and they were worried in case they let the side down. Others were afraid they would lose their friends by being associated with Open Doors and so lose an opportunity of sharing the Christian faith more naturally in other ways.

'Christ said that we must take up our cross and follow him,' I urged, 'but he did not mean that it is a burden. Relax! It's not your job to convert the world. You don't have to explain all the mysteries of God's action in the world. What electrician can explain all the mysteries of electricity? What he does is to do what he knows he can do. Your job and mine is to share what we have discovered about God and let him do the rest.'

Perhaps the most important thing about Open Doors was its value in getting members of the congregation to use their homes and in developing their confidence in speaking about their faith. One of our mature members said to me in great delight, 'You know, I actually told my neighbour about my Christian faith today! He said to me, "Thank you for the supper party last night. I didn't know until then that you were religious. Have you always been associated with the church?" I said a quick prayer for the Holy Spirit to fill me with love and I found myself actually talking about the Christian faith. And he is going to come to church. Isn't that terrific?' It was indeed terrific that

Christians, like that man, were beginning to relate their faith to their jobs and their communities.

As Easter Day approached, so our final Gift Day, approached as well. All along we had planned that Easter 1982 would be our very last Gift Day and after that there would be no more appeals for money. We started our giving on Easter Day 1980 and we felt that it was right to make Easter 1982 the end of the Project. The cost of the project had now risen to £325,000—this we were assured was the final figure. We had about £90,000 to go. All we could do was to remind the congregation of the need to finish the Project once and for all. We had grown so used to God's amazing interventions that, having prayed about it, we knew we could lean on his abundant resources in Christ.

Easter Day arrived and once again we had wonderful services of praise and celebration. There was a feeling of peace about the need to finish the project, and no sense of urgency or crisis prevailed. At the end of the day to an expectant congregation we were able to announce that £80,000 had been given, bringing the total to £315,000—just £10,000 short. A wonderful amount towards a truly staggering total—but not enough.

Some of our leaders were very disappointed. 'We are so close, but not there yet—what can we do?' was the cry. But we had given our word—there would be no more Gift Days or appeals. If God had proved his faithfulness to us in the past, we knew we could trust him for the rest.

And he provided. Over the next few months prior to our leaving the rest of the money came in, so that when we left, the Project was completely paid for. Many members of the congregation would say that the money was 'prayed in' because no further announcements were made about it. In just over two years therefore the task was finished. In spite of many worries and anxieties, at no point had we been in debt. From a congregation which, humanly speaking, could not raise such a prodigious amount, God had confounded us all by providing through us. His bounty and goodness outstripped our wildest expectations.

On the evening before Eileen and I and our four children left to move to Trinity College, I visited the church for the last time and I did two things.

First of all I wandered around the church for a little while, taking in all the changes and thinking back over the seven years we had been here. I found myself asking: 'How did all this happen?' The answer came in the memories flooding back. At the heart of it all was God's faithfulness to us. We had discovered this at moments of weakness and fear and we had discovered the real power of prayer. In spite of our weakness, he had never let us down. We had sailed very close to the wind, but the fragile craft of faith had survived. But the project was also about harnessing the resources of the whole congregation; we had all worked together so closely that it was truly the achievement of the whole body of Christ. And I gave thanks for the commitment of this renewed people who had given so sacrificially.

Then, as I reflected further, I thanked God the Holy Spirit for giving gifts for service and ministry. Although there was still much for us to experience of spiritual gifts and graces, there was now a sense of expectancy in the congregation which made them excitingly open to a new future. As I stood there in the church I thought back to the painful changes in worship which had precipitated many of the changes that followed. And I thanked God for the joy, freedom and life we had experienced together in worship, and I prayed that this would continue and develop. Last of all, I thought about the wonder of the Christian life and the power of Christ to keep each Christian, and I prayed that this congregation would never lose the thrill of following Jesus of Nazareth to his cross and experiencing with him the newness of his resurrection.

The last thing I did in the building that evening was to talk and pray with a man who wanted to know more about the Christian faith. It was strangely symbolic that the very last thing I did in my ministry at St Nicholas's Church was to talk to someone about the Christian faith.

But then, that's what it's all about—isn't it?